Praise for *The CEO Difference*

"Advancing in your career is all about differentiating yourself from others around you. No one teaches that lesson better than D. A. [Debra] Benton, and she teaches it nowhere better than in *The CEO Difference*."

—**Rulon F. Stacey**, PhD, FACHE, President and Chief Executive Officer, Fairview Health Services, and Chairman of the Board of Overseers for the Malcolm Baldrige National Quality Award

"New books arrive on my desk just about every day, but I always read the books of D. A. Benton."

—**Brian Palmer**, President, National Speakers Bureau

"Playing well with others is one of the mysteries of corporate life, but how to do this better than anyone else has been solved for you. All you have to do is listen closely to one of the greatest corporate mystery analysts of all time: D. A. Benton has written a masterful book on solving this universal case study."

—**Jack Falvey**, contributor to *Barron's* and the *Wall Street Journal* and founder of MakingTheNumbers.Com

"No matter your title or industry, you need to stand out in order to be successful in today's competitive business landscape. The challenge is often identifying how. In this book, D. A. Benton shares important key behaviors she observed from working with Fortune 500 senior executives around the world that can have a profound impact on anyone's career."

—**Rick Ambrose**, Executive Vice President, Lockheed Martin Space Systems Company

"The secret to recognition and success is revealed in *The CEO Difference*, as D. A. Benton clearly and concisely guides the aspiring executive to stand out in a crowd and avoid the herd instinct. A must-read for any ambitious man or woman striving to reach the next rung on the organization ladder. You have what it takes. Now you will know how to package and sell yourself and your programs. It's easy . . . once you learn the secret!"

—**John Bianchi**, PhD, founder and CEO, Bianchi International (retired), Commanding General of the California State Military Reserve, author of *Blue Steel and Gunleather*, and founder of Frontier Gunleather

"In today's intensely competitive arena, career success requires much more than brains, skills, and perseverance. In *The CEO Difference*, Debra has distilled powerful, easy-to-apply lessons to set yourself apart from the competition as you plan, create, and act. Well worth the read."

—**M. Carl Johnson, III**, Group Executive Vice President and Chief Growth Officer, Del Monte Foods

"CEOs and other persons with high-level authority and responsibility have achieved success not only by being different but by making that difference count in creating productivity and prosperity across their the organizations. This achievement is not a unilateral adventure but a focused regime with a network of internal and external influences that challenges one to define their value above others."

—**Herbert R. Temple Jr.**, Lieutenant General, U.S. Army (retired)

"Benton knows the correct pathway to move into CEO leadership. This book has motivational tools for all stages in climbing into the CEO chair or to change the mindset and steps of climbers who seek their peak performance."

—**Laurence Salmon**, CEO, RJPD Asset Management Singapore

"If what you are looking for is a way to the top through your own actions, this is the book for you. It provides great insight into how to understand yourself and to project your best self to the outside world."

—**James J. O'Brien**, Chairman and CEO, Ashland Inc.

"Benton's insights are so invaluable that they extend past the professional sphere and into my personal life. She is a wonderful woman with profound knowledge and unparalleled expertise."

—**Sibylle Scherer**, President, Consumer Marketing and Branding/DFS GROUP (duty free shops)

"Once again Benton has captured the essence of what CEOs are looking for and 'see' in those we want leading our companies. In a highly competitive world and changing marketplace, the demands for leadership differentiation are as high as for the products we sell. This book certainly provides an insightful treatment on how to achieve and be recognized as one of those few leaders."

—**Larry A. Lawson**, CEO, Spirit Aero Systems, Inc.

"Smarts and hard work have become commodities in our competitive economy—they are necessary just to do an 'acceptable' job. Getting even smarter and working even harder has let many climb the next step. At this point, however, few are left with the passion and energy to become 'exceptional.' To get there, you'll have to do something different. Benton shows you how and why!"

—**Dr. Dino Falaschetti**, Executive Director, PERC (Property and Environment Research Center), and former Senior Economist for the President's Council of Economic Advisers

"When I mentor many of my exceptional associates, we discuss how to distinguish ourselves in the appropriate ways among other peers who are 'exceed-ers' as well. Debra has been my coach for many years, and she has again provided clear and succinct advice and techniques to advance in your career."

—**Michael Gass**, President and CEO, United Launch Alliance

"For those intent on accelerating their move up the career ladder, D. A. Benton's newest book provides an invaluable 'decoder ring' that unlocks the secrets for making the 'High Potential!' lights burn brightly whenever the people you work for see your name.

Reaching the top doesn't happen by accident; it happens to people who distinguish themselves . . . and this is a smart place to learn how to do it."

—**Hal Johnson**, Chairman, Global Human Resources
Practice, Korn/Ferry International

"The guide to success for corporate as well as public service officials is well described in Debra Benton's new how-to book, *The CEO Difference*, for ambitious men and women on the way up in their organizations. Great suggestions never before presented are well illustrated. This is an easy read, well worth the time, and a very important addition to your library!"

—**Dave Snowden**, Chief of Police, Beverly Hills, CA

THE CEO DIFFERENCE

HOW TO CLIMB, CRAWL, AND LEAP YOUR WAY
TO THE NEXT LEVEL OF YOUR CAREER

D. A. BENTON

New York   Chicago   San Francisco   Athens   London   Madrid
Mexico City   Milan   New Delhi   Singapore   Sydney   Toronto

1 2 3 4 5 6 7 8 9 0   DOC/DOC   1 9 8 7 6 5 4

ISBN 978-0-07-182833-8
MHID 0-07-182833-8

e-ISBN 978-0-07-182835-2
e-MHID 0-07-182835-4

Library of Congress Cataloging-in-Publication Data
Benton, D. A. (Debra A.)
    The CEO difference : how to climb, crawl, and leap your way to the next level of your career / D. A. Benton.
        pages cm
    ISBN-13: 978-0-07-182833-8 (hardback)
    ISBN-10: 0-07-182833-8 (hardback)
1. Executive ability. 2. Chief executive officers. 3. Leadership. I. Title.
    HD38.2.B462 2014
    658.4'2—dc23

                                                           2013041724

McGraw-Hill Education books are available at special quantity discounts to use as premiums and sales promotions or for use in corporate training programs. To contact a representative, please visit the Contact Us pages at www.mhprofessional.com.

■

**To my mom and dad, Teresa and Fred Benton,
who sadly have passed; and to my
cowboy, Rodney Sweeney**

■

CONTENTS

PART III: HOW TO DIFFERENTIATE YOUR ACTIONS

ACKNOWLEDGMENTS

I WANT TO give a special thank-you to Curtis Rex Carter, CEO of America, Inc., one of the smartest businessmen I know. And to my wise and patient editor, Zachary Gajewski, and my trusted and always good-natured assistant, Laura Althorpe.

I've always tried to surround myself with people "pages ahead of me" in the instruction manual of life. At every step in my career, I've made a point to have a personal advisory and sounding board of people who inspire, guide, teach, edify, enlighten, and entertain. They answer my questions with candor and give advice whether I asked for it or not. To these brilliant, fun, and accomplished people, I want to say thank you.

Tetsuya Abe
Rick Ambrose
Ron Arvine
Carol Ballock
Mike Barkley
Andrew R. Basile, Jr.
Devon Beitzel
Bernard Berkin
Daryl Brewster
Corinne Joy Brown
Henrique Moreira Campos
Karen Castranova
Cynthia Christie
Sharon Clinebell
Eric Cole
Doug Conant
Todd Dewett
Mohammad Elesiah
Brian Fabes
Dr. Dino Falaschetti
Rebecca Feaster
Christopher Felder
Bradley Fortin
Joel Goeltl
Kristin Golliher
Rick Griggs
Kerry Hansen
Dave Hardie
Jerry Henry
Mario Hernandez

Mike Hernandez

Robert Herron

Kerry Hicks

Ernie Horne

Carl Johnson

Hal Johnson

Chet Kapoor

Donna Karaba

Kelvin Kesler

Natalie Laackman

Laurence Land

Larry Lawson

Steve Mangum

Peter Mannetti

Don Mann

Ray Martinez

Jim McBride

Garrett McNamara

Troy Miles

Karen Mitchal

Mike Moniz

Mark Moulton

Deanna Mulligan

Dan Munroe

Adil Nemat

Heidi Olinger

Ken Olson

Rick Owens

Elizabeth Parra

Katy Piotrowski

Hal Pittman

Bruce Razbun

Mary Margaret Reed

Tim Riley

Ken Roper

Laurence Salmon

Allison Saltzer

Susan Schell

Paul Schlossberg

Ray Scott

Chris Seegers

Angela Setter

Sandra Shoemaker

Karen Marie Simmons

Greg Smith

Nathan Teegarden

Ricard Toeppe

Michale Trufant

T. J. Walker

Sandra Walston

Michael Warring

Samantha Weinstein

Kurt Wiese

Philip Wilkinson

Kevin Willis

Lew Wymeisner

Carl Yankowski

Leo Zuckerman

Jared Carr and his Proship Acceleration Program crew: Mollie Bonner, Callie Chamberlain, Sean Flaherty, Andrew Guggenberger, Lisa Klass, Blake Koch, Paul Lillehaugen, Kelsie Lungstrom, Betsy Nolan, Aaron Opheim, Drew Penz, Greta Peterson, Brittany Quinn, Nicole Radil, Jonathan Rangoonwala, Grant Severson, Mark Stockhowe, Jr., Benjamin Stumph, Emiliano Urbina, and Jordan Williamson.

INTRODUCTION

I KNOW YOU'RE a solid citizen. You're a quick learner and truly smart. You try hard. You're pretty cool. You get along with people. You set a respectable example. You want to help and connect with others, to serve society. You aim to contribute meaningful work. You have dreams and goals to achieve something groundbreaking. You're motivated by money, title, and power to a certain extent, but you are more motivated by growth opportunities and success for your kids.

You plan to accelerate your career growth *quickly*—to play full out, use all your talent, and bring something to the world it hasn't had before.

And—*at least on paper*—you are just like every other ambitious individual.

Let me ask you: Who couldn't say those things about himself or herself? That list of career aspirations is remarkably alike and interchangeable for almost everyone. It's acceptable but not exceptional.

Today, you have to exceed in a group of exceed-*ers*. As fine as you are and as well as you're doing, you can do better—so people will want to promote you, conduct business with you, follow you, and recommend you to others.

Even if you are the "best in class," your competition is good too. Percentage-wise there aren't too many lousy, slacker workers in corporate America. According to a recent United Nations report, U.S. employees beat all 27 nations in the European Union, Japan, and Switzerland in productivity. You're around a lot of competent people across companies, functions, and jobs who are thinking and doing the same thing in their career as you are doing in yours. Added to that are plenty of excellent people coming around the corner. Aside from the natural need to earn a living, their main goal is similar to yours: to do enjoyable, creative work and flourish in the world.

Talents and dreams are quite universal. What you do with them is not.

Differentiate Yourself Big Time

If you want to be übermarketable and have a potent impact not only in your life and career but with everyone around you, you have to set yourself apart from every other overachiever with whom you compete. You can't just putt-putt around.

Why? Because there is no second chance! This is your one life to live. Isn't that reason enough? What's more, people who excel always do things differently from others. And those who differentiate themselves find that they are performing better in all aspects of life. Keep in mind:

- That's how your boss chooses whom to promote among comparably talented people.
- When all candidates look good on paper, this difference is what recruiters look for.
- No matter your age, someone younger (and likely less expensive) is ready to push you aside.
- Today's technology is constantly advancing, allowing more people to compete with you globally.

One new manager told me this: "The stakes are even higher with a virtual workplace. I see my boss once a week, not every day, and I can't leave anything to chance." With today's ongoing advancements in technology, you're competing with more talent than at any time in history—and not just in the United States but also in China, India, Mexico, Africa, Japan, Brazil, and about 145 other countries.

The digital world makes a rightful meritocracy. If you do souped-up work as a way to differentiate yourself among your competitors, you'll win out. It doesn't matter where you come from, who you are, or who you know.

Though most people like to believe they are singular, unique, and one-of-a kind in their assignments, few are. Across the world we are more similar than dissimilar. Yet, as fate would have it, your boss is looking for someone singular, who outshines the rest.

You see, right now, private conversations are taking place in secret sessions. Behind closed doors with shades drawn, management muckity-mucks sitting in high-back leather chairs are thinking hard about you and a smattering of your competitors. One person is enthusiastically singled out with the confirmatory statement, "He's different." Someone asks, "What do you mean?" and the muckity-muck answers, "He fits in, but he stands out from the rest too. He does more, gets more out of others, knows more, cares more, and *is* more."

Those few words carry significant ramifications in your work life, usurping the university you attended, companies you've worked for, titles you've held, and any other personal or professional pedigree attached to you.

Not everyone is going to be able to move up. Company leaders are scrutinizing your skills and talent, performance, and results. They are looking at the continuous competitive advantage you furnish the organization and the effect you have on others. You want to be the one to leave an "echo beyond the room," meaning the one about whom the conversation keeps going after she has left the scene. As one female friend put it, "The often quoted Coco Chanel said it well: 'In order to be irreplaceable, one must always be different.'"

There is a lot you can't control in life, but there are ways in which you can exert more echo:

- Find what differentiates you.
- Do regular things in a different way.
- Do different things than your competitors do.

All of those actions will add value as you contend.

A *Forbes* article by Karl Moore (January 28, 2013) reported on the three stages of a career: the first is establishing relationships and gaining know-how; the second stage is differentiating yourself; and the third is passing it on. My only argument is that the "differentiating" needs to be in all three stages from the beginning to the end. If it's not in the first, how will you stand out from others doing the same thing? And if you don't do it in the last stage, who is going to want to learn from you?

You cannot produce average, mediocre, lackluster results at any stage in your career, or you will be forever racing to catch up. You have to fight extra hard to *more than* just measure up. If you take the position that all you want is just to hang on to your job, you won't be in the game long.

FOUR CEOs ON DIFFERENTIATING YOURSELF

Daryl Brewster, CEO of the Committee Encouraging Corporate Philanthropy (CECP) and formerly the CEO of Krispy Kreme and the president of Nabisco:

> You can meet results and exceed expectations. You can gain experiences that fill a gap. You can be relevant. But you must still find a way to differentiate yourself through your performance and your leadership to advance your career.

Reid Hoffman, LinkedIn cofounder:

> How are you first, only, faster, better, or cheaper than other people who want to do what you're doing in the world? What are you offering that's hard to come by? What are you offering that's both rare and valuable?

John Krebbs, president of Krebbs & Associates, formerly the CEO of PAC:

> If you have a message to deliver, it gets lost if no one sees you, knows you, or notices you. You get lost too, being part of a crowd.

Peter Mannetti, managing partner of iSherpa Capital:

> Because iSherpa is a venture capitalist firm, people come to us with ideas all the time. The people who stand out are engaging, and they create mutual understanding. They paint a vision you can grasp and a clear next step that moves you from skepticism to collaboration. Recently I met a 28-year-old who had just sold his business and was starting a new company. I joined his board because he caught my eye. He has a special "quality" about him. He is a college dropout, obviously self-educated, but he can talk about all kinds of things. He asks thoughtful questions, then makes good statements full of interesting ideas. Plus he is fun to be around; he isn't full of himself. He engages you, and he is the type who causes me to say, "I want this person on my team."

Interchangeable Is Replaceable

To differentiate is not to one-up, grandstand, show off, or beat someone else for personal gain. It's to surpass where you were yesterday, last week, and last year. It's being distinct to make a difference.

To stand out from the pack, you don't have to be 6 feet 8 inches tall, wear your clothes inside out, be a blonde Norwegian working in South Texas, or be a loud, obnoxious extrovert. You don't have to get another advanced degree, work a 14-hour day, labor eight days a week, lose weight, change the color of your hair, or name your first-born after your boss.

You can be modest, self-effacing, hardworking, quiet, and effective. Just do a little more, a little better in a multitude of areas to be both rare and valuable. Fortunately, you'll find it's not that difficult.

One CEO I interviewed spoke to me about an employee who started out working for the catering company that supplied the corporate cafeteria. The man had immigrated to this country in hopes of providing more opportunity for his family. The job he got was as a food server for the corporate caterer. But he didn't just ladle soup or drop chicken strips on a paper plate. He did more. He stood tall with pride; he wasn't hunched over, oppressed, or grumpy-looking. He was friendly with everyone coming down the line, including the serious-faced executives. He smiled at them, even if they didn't smile back, and he remembered their names. He put in the extra effort to offer samples to taste before the executives made a food choice. He could recall favorite foods they liked, and he would point out, "Mr. __, I noticed you liked the cucumber salad, and we have that again today." Or "Did you see that we have fresh, local sliced peaches?"

He always went the extra mile and a half, including being particularly neat in his grooming, even wearing a suit and tie every day, which was not the typical server dress, and he did not wear "business casual" on Fridays. Frankly, he dressed like the senior executives dressed. During his work break, he would roam the area instead of retreating to the kitchen, checking to see if someone needed a drink refill or a second helping. Even though the setup was largely self-serve, he continued to be of service. He would go to the cafeteria attendant, bring her a beverage or dessert treat, and even offer to run errands for her, make copies, or deliver packages throughout the office building.

Whenever his name came up in front of and behind closed doors, it was always with, "Isn't he great!"

The company ended up changing catering vendors, but the employees didn't want to lose this particular server so they petitioned to keep him on, resulting in the man's getting the newly created job of manager of the corporate cafeteria—a big step from being a vendor's server. His behavior created a career for himself that included benefits and a pension—something he hadn't had before. When Superstorm Sandy ravaged the corporate headquarters resulting in people being temporarily laid off, everyone insisted he remain on. The CEO told me, "He has the most job security in the entire company, even more than I have."

Most people will read the above paragraphs and think, "That's nice," but few will decide to take it upon themselves to consistently do more and do more, better. To distinguish yourself from all the other also-rans, be in that elite group who will do more.

Your boss won't have to be a member of Mensa to see the difference.

It's Not Too Early or Too Late

You have to continue to differentiate yourself at each stage in your career. Regardless of your age, at every point in your life, there is a younger person eager to step into your job. If you are 30 years old, there is an impatient 20-something coming up on you; at 40 there is that pesky 30-year-old. One 60-year-old CEO told me about a 44-year-old knocking on his door to take over the company—his own son!

The problem is that you, like others, had the impetus to "do something" and "be someone" when you started your career, but then the realities of life set in with marriages, children, divorces, debts, illnesses, and career hiccups. Then someone "sped up the clock" when you weren't watching, and now a bleak picture frequently pops up of you aging fast in an outdated building, lined with long rows of gray cubicles, and you are pushing paper and working in a mundane and mind-numbing job, with no excitement or significance.

Put all that real life together, and it can become a little discouraging. It could make you question yourself or even give up, disengage, chuck it all, and drop out. But you can't because you have responsibilities, pride, dreams, hopes, and the need to prove to yourself you *do* have it in you to create an extremely meaningful personal and professional existence.

When you want something you've never had, you have to do something you've never done. Whatever your age, job situation, work history, or family way, turn up the juice going forward. Do it now, do it for your team, your company, and yourself—that is, unless you are ready to give up. But if you are like me, *you aren't about to give up.* You must realize that personal reinvention never ends whether you have a little gray hair or no hair.

This book is not about selfishly ratcheting yourself up the ladder. Instead, I'm writing about how to be a success. It's not just your advancement plan we're dealing with but the advancement of your team, group, and organization. You distinguish yourself by constantly asking these questions: How can I outdo others who could fill the role? What more can I do for the team? How can I add extra value to my boss's work? What could I do next to be more useful to my colleagues? Where can I improve that helps my boss's boss and the whole business?

You're not going to fall into your future. You're going to have to climb, crawl, and leap in. As Warren Buffett said in his 2013 annual meeting for Berkshire Hathaway, "You want restlessness, a feeling that somebody's always after you, but you're going to stay ahead."

If your career hasn't been as stellar as you expected, here's your chance for a second shot, a do-over, a new start, a second wind, another take. If this is your first time at bat, great; if you've been there and want to do it again, wonderful. If you're looking for one last hurrah, that's cool too.

To have a great life and an electrifying career, you have to distinguish yourself from a lot of good people. You need to continue to prove your own mettle and influence other people to do likewise. You have to turn it up a notch, go all out. If you aren't distinct and separate, your boss will find someone who is.

A Career Reality Check

Smart people do stupid things all the time when they forget that, at this moment, the next new big thing is coming around the corner, chasing them. In that situation, frankly, the less talented individual will win out if she or he has more fight. If you think your personal brilliance will keep you above the fray, you're wrong. If you think none of this affects you yet, you're wrong again.

How you decide to act in the next few minutes will decide the person you're going to be from now on. So shut the door, ignore unsolicited e-mails, and let the phone calls go to voice mail.

A PERSONAL RELEVANCE REALITY CHECK

Take a moment for a personal relevance reality check because at any age these painful things can start happening to you, and if they do, you'll want to change your course of behavior:

- You increasingly feel that your smarts aren't getting you anywhere, that your skills aren't being used.

- You aren't sought out or taken seriously by colleagues and managers.
- You sense disregard for your authority by those above, below, or around you.
- You can't seem to gain new responsibilities, and your current ones are being chipped away.
- Your honest self-assessment tells you that your expertise doesn't always fit present-day needs; you aren't "with it."
- Your ideas to improve work aren't welcome.
- You experience notable indignities, such as being ignored in meetings, being left out of the loop on key decisions, or being omitted from the circulation lists from important e-mails, meetings, and social gatherings.
- You get heavy and steady criticism of your work.
- You are frequently passed over for the most interesting, important, or prestigious assignments.

All of these things can happen if you allow them to happen. But you, my dear reader, will not let this happen. You've got the fight in you, or you are ready to get it back if you've let it slip.

Right now, take your age in years and multiply it by 365. That's how many days you are old. Whether you are 10,220 days old or 21,275 days old, it's only one single day that makes a change in your life, not a year. Each one of your days has a start, a morning, noon, night, and an end. You have to vow to yourself to make something of the 1,440 minutes you have each day. Take just a few of those minutes, and use them to put effort into doing things a little out of the ordinary, a little beyond anyone else's efforts. Don't put this book down until you can take away one idea or thought to distinguish yourself in whatever situation you are currently in *today*. The truth is, not everyone will follow that advice, but if you do, then you're already starting to set yourself apart.

The Ultimate Goal

My purpose is to help you master the what, how, and why of productively distinguishing yourself from other great people—to benefit both your organization and you.

I went to some of the best CEOs and C-level executives in the country and asked these questions: "What causes you to positively notice an employee when you hire or promote?" "What is a big separator to you between comparably talented people?" "What did *you* do to differentiate yourself in your own career?"

From those conversations, I found numerous traits that cause individuals to stand out from the crowd—traits that will be discussed at length in the following chapters. Any one of them might be enough to move you to the next level, but if you have all of them, you are certain to have separators on steroids (the good kind). You'll be off the charts as you leap ahead further and faster than your competition.

There is no one template for every job, of course. One CEO told me, "I *don't want* a creative risk-taking accountant." But another said, "I *want* an innovative, risk-taking accountant."

You'll find everything is in the eye of the beholder.

With any of the differentiating traits, you have to leave the ordinary behind, maybe buck the system a little, or at least not go where the crowd goes, regardless of your age or current success. Just as companies must constantly change and evolve, so must you. Steve Ballmer, formerly the CEO of Microsoft, speaking at a corporate conference, described how companies achieve more success: "You either move ahead, or you go away."

Those eight words apply to you as well. Think of running your career like running a business. You are the commander in chief of your career, the captain of your industry, and the CEO of your life.

At every juncture in your career, you have to fight to keep ahead. And by "fight" I don't mean food or fists flung or flying barstools. I mean you don't slack off, use half-measures, play it safe, or be commonplace and ordinary—because someone will eat your lunch if you do!

If you don't stay competitive, you're going to have a problem moving you and your group forward.

If you don't initiate, stand up, step up, and step out, someone else will. If you're not prominent, you're going to blend in, and, frankly, blending in is the worst thing you can do for your career.

To be different and better, you have to work full on and flat out, fire on all cylinders, stand out, get ahead of the curve, and be all in. As the saying goes, "Lead or get out of the way." The beauty is, it only requires more thought and energy than others are willing to put to it—and that's not hard to do.

My aim with this book is to make the extra effort and attention that you put into setting yourself apart as uncomplicated and doable as possible. My approach is anticomplexity. I'm taking the mystery out of the dance. My focus is on helping you in being:

- Authentic in what makes you special.
- Capable of successfully and effectively communicating your offerings across a diverse organization, team, or tribe.
- Able to use your distinction for your own career acceleration and satisfaction.
- Skilled in using what you learn to achieve something larger than yourself.

Let me be clear: when you differentiate yourself, your goal is not to be a nonconformist, a rebel, a misfit, or a showoff; nor is it for you to be contrary, arrogant, and strange. It is not for your personal ego lift. Rather, it is for you to be part of something bigger than you.

Distinguishing yourself is meant to help you break the mold, modify what exists, and disrupt patterns for more effective outcomes in your personal and professional life.

Not everyone will follow this advice; not everyone can. But *you* aren't everyone, are you?

Why Am I So Passionate About This Simple Philosophy?

Because I've seen it make a measurable difference in people's lives, including my own.

I was raised in an average middle-class, mid-America family of small business owners. Both of my parents and most of my relatives had some sort of business in which they were the boss (for example, grocery store, drug store, farm, ranch, or dress shop). Around the dinner table, they always talked about their work, and from a young age I noticed that they were always trying and succeeding in doing things a little differently. It was a challenge for them to always vary and alter what they offered, how they presented, and what they did to contend with their competitors (friends and foes). Doing more was a constant in their lives, and it was necessary to survive financially. They weren't paragons of perfection, but their example gave me permission to be different at a young age, at a time in life when most kids try to be the same as each other. It became second nature for me to seek out the seldom-tried or unusual approach.

I took flying lessons before I was old enough to get my driver's license, competed in pageants at the height of bra-burning feminism, wore short hair and dresses when all the girls wore long hair and jeans, and worked at a radio station so the disc jockeys would help me study for my FCC broadcast license. From junior high on, I earned my own spending money from various sales jobs, and by age 13, I was managing two girls who were working for me.

I graduated from Colorado State University in 1974 with a four-year degree in economics that I had earned in three years. I chose to major in economics at the last minute while I was in the registration line because I noticed that all males were signed up for that subject. It wasn't that I was boy crazy or that I had any special interest in economics. I chose it for two reasons: (1) I felt that men still largely controlled the business world, and it would be important to learn what they were learning, and (2) I wanted to do things differently than the other female students.

My education was always what I wanted it to be. I never lusted for advanced degrees, and instead I jumped head on into my calling: starting my own career consulting company two years after graduation. Someone described the move at the time as "an act of desperation to do something productive." I hired the experienced talent necessary to conduct the consulting, and I ran the business part as I constantly fed my curiosity, read, talked to other business owners, introduced new ideas, observed how successful leaders worked, and experimented to develop my own niche.

It dawned on me early in my career that the top of the business world would be the best place to learn from, over academics (although there's nothing wrong with that route). I had read an old Chinese proverb: "A single conversation across the table with a wise man is worth a month's study of books." So I decided to learn from the best in business. I ended up sitting "across the table" for 30 years, interviewing, shadowing (not stalking), developing friendships with, and gaining mentoring relationships with some Fortune 100 and 500 company CEOs and executives; some entrepreneurs through the Young Presidents' Organization, the Young Entrepreneurs' Organization, and the World Business Organization; some politicians in the Washington Beltway; and some highly placed people in the global community. My goal was to find out what those successful leaders and executives did to make it to the top of their profession as compared to comparably talented coworkers so that I could both use that information for myself and teach it to others in turn.

The common thread I discovered was that they had succeeded in distinguishing themselves from other people as good as they were.

So I started coaching CEOs, CEO wannabes, and C-suite executives. I consulted for companies about lessons that I had from those interviews. Condé Nast *Portfolio* magazine named me one of the "top 5 executive coaches to have on speed dial." Topceocoaches.com listed me as one of the "world's top 10 CEO coaches." I wrote my first book, titled *Lions Don't Need to Roar*, and it was published in 1991. I thought I was a one-time author, but when a book sells well, the publisher wants you to do another. So in 1994, *How to Think Like a CEO* was published. It became a *New York Times* business bestseller, which resulted in my writing a series of other books such as *Secrets of a CEO Coach, Executive Charisma*, and *CEO Material*, including my most recent *The Virtual Executive* (McGraw-Hill, 2012). Each book was a reinvention of my expertise to fit the times and provide value to my readers, clients, and speaking audiences.

Today I coach executives in 19 different countries around the world, and I present keynote speeches before associations and business audiences of many Fortune 500 companies with audiences ranging from hundreds to thousands. My speaking venues have included the U.S. Border Patrol, the Crystal Cathedral, Wall Street firms, and the U.S.S. *Clark* missile frigate. I've worked with two U.S. presidential candidates, as well as a number of congressional candidates and a few gubernatorial contenders. I've advised executives in their careers to interview with Donald Trump, to present at the Academy Awards, to testify before Senate hearings, and to accept a Nobel Peace Prize.

For this book I want to explain the secrets I've learned from some of the smartest businesspeople in the world. These secrets can help you achieve sustained success and help you either jump-start your career or leapfrog ahead of your competition.

The one overriding theme in the answers to the questions I posed in my interviews was this: "Be different and better than others in everything you do." So then I asked, "How and why?" Now I'm giving those answers to you.

A NOTE TO MY READERS

To write this book, I went to CEOs, C-suite executives, and gurus who have differing areas of expertise. Some are from my own board of advisors and mentors of 10, 20, and 30 years; others are clients, colleagues, and friends whose success I applaud. They generously offered me experienced opinions on what makes an individual stand out from the group when they hire and promote.

They all had this in common: a willingness to be straight with me *for your* benefit, to "call it like it is" regarding work life today.

In this book, sometimes I attributed quotes to particular people by name, but usually not. Sometimes a comment was made in a public venue, and so I felt comfortable attaching a person's name to it. But just as often, a great statement or story came from a private conversation or coaching session. I felt the example would be helpful so I included it, but I also wanted to respect the privacy of the person speaking.

In a conversation with a CEO that I sat beside on a long flight from Hong Kong to Bangkok, he said: "Name names. You'll make a lot of money, but you might have to move out of the country." I chose not to move.

A different situation that I have encountered in previous books I've written in which I've attributed quotes to named individuals—for example, on job hunting advice—is that hundreds of readers wrote to the CEO whose name I mentioned using his advice, and they expected a job. Some people actually got snarky with me and the CEO for not following what was written despite the applicants' not having the necessary qualifications.

My goal is to provide you candid, honest, straight-from-the-horse's-mouth advice, but I also want to be upright with the people helping you and me.

The CEOs and C-suite executives that I talked to for this book come from the following organizations, listed in alphabetical order: Anchor Brewing, Apple, AT&T, Avis, Campbell's Soup, Chevron, Coors, DuPont, Gatorade, GE, Gillette, Godiva, Google, J.Crew, Johns-Manville, Jordan Vineyards, Kraft, Korn/Ferry, Lockheed Martin, Microsoft, New York Stock Exchange, Newmont Mining, Pepperidge Farm, Pfizer, PricewaterhouseCoopers, Quaker Oats, Seattle Mariners, Steinway, Time-Warner, Toyota, United Airlines, United Artists Entertainment, United Healthcare, Verizon, Viacom, Walt Disney Company, and Yahoo!. Some interviewees came from other companies that aren't household names but are equally well run: America, Inc., American Education Products, Arvine Pipe & Supply Company, Big Enterprises, Brookside Management, Chicago's Civic Consulting Alliance, Daniels Cablevision, Dilenschneider Group, Feaster & Associates, Hight Performance Group, Krebbs &

Associates, Mac Daddy Enterprises, Merry X-Ray, Portsmouth & Associates, Wilfley & Sons, and several others.

Everything I write about is what I learned from these qualified people to pass on to you. Just as you want to be exceptional, they want more exceptional people to recruit and promote. One CEO told me this: "There isn't a pool of talent out there. It's more like a puddle, and if this book can increase the size, I'm all in."

You can be assured that the advice comes from exceptional people who care about you because I care about you.

This is what I can tell you to help you have an exceptional, fun, exciting, happy, fulfilling life—for you, the children that you parent, and the people that you influence in life.

You *Own* Your Career, Life, and Legacy

In life there are few things you can control. You can view that fact with anxiety or with exhilaration that the unpredictability and uncertainty are what make it fun.

Still, you want to take ownership of what you can in your career. You're never a finished product. If you choose, you can always learn. You can always have an opportunity to make something you'll be proud of the rest of your life.

Make your mind up, and then do something about your decision to distinguish yourself in all aspects of how you think, act, and work.

As Brian Fabes, CEO of Chicago's Civic Consulting Alliance, says: "If a leader isn't reaching toward big goals, which is core to getting ahead, he or she will soon find himself or herself behind. In Satchel Page's words, 'Someone might be gaining.' I met a former CEO on a bike trip this fall. He told me his motto was 'Run scared.' I would add, 'But don't let them see you're scared,' so the core message is the same. Don't stop striving, reaching, running."

You're on your own, and it's all up to you. But it *is* there for *you*, so go hard like an Ironman athlete. And yes, there is stress in being a go-getter, always attempting to grow and evolve. However, there is also significant stress, even depression, in a humdrum, going-nowhere, doing-nothing way of life.

Kevin Willis, CFO for Ashland, has this to say on the topic:

> The way I look at my career, I'm managing a business of one. I've always looked at it that way. So I ask myself the question, "What differentiates me from my competition?" At least once per year, I take stock—that's what I call it. This is typically over the holidays. I think about where I stand, what I've done to create competitive advantage for myself, and I develop ideas and objectives to execute over the coming year. In short, I'm really intentional about it. I think about it because it matters to me. I've managed my career for years because it became apparent that if I didn't, others would gladly manage it for me, to their own benefit.

Some companies hire people with five years' work experience who graduated with an MBA from a top-tier American business school such as Harvard or Wharton. These companies then put these employees through a process of two-year job rotations—four assignments of six months each—to allow them to hone what they want to do in the company. You may have missed the boat on such a program, but you can initiate your own.

Today, darn it, your company can't afford to train and develop you the way you deserve. It's up to you to do it. Besides, the company couldn't fully provide what works for you anyway. You have to create your own version of that. Bob Berkowitz, a partner in the Dilenschneider & Company and formerly a White House correspondent for NBC News, told me what he does: "Every day, several times a day, I ask myself these few questions: 'What new idea, insight, or clarification can I read, learn, or unearth that will help me be different and better? And how can I connect my talent, ability, what I love to do, and what I'm good at to help others get what they want?' It's me training my brain to be hyperaware and conscious."

Success is about intention, belief, and action. The more energy you put in to exercising this "muscle," the more results you'll get.

So let's start cultivating your own greatness because if you're not moving forward, you're slipping behind. And we don't want that.

With persistence and imagination, one person can change the world—at least your world—and that is you. As Michael Warring, president of American Educational Products, said to me: "Each individual is responsible for either accepting or changing his or her own situation." It's that simple. And with extra effort, you just might find yourself at the top of your game.

Nobody can stop you from getting better. Just as you constantly update your clothes, your car, and your hairstyle, update yourself. We're all created equal, but some of us find a way to rise above the herd so as not to end up lost in it. As one CEO put it, "Debra, you help people train for living: the Olympics of life."

PART I

How to Differentiate Your Thinking

CHAPTER 1

Be Self-Confident

MORE THAN intelligence, experience, skill, or talent, self-confidence is the most essential element in life. Pretty strong statement, right? Well, think about it. If you are extremely smart, experienced, skilled, and talented, and you have the greatest idea, but you are too timid or hesitant to step up and speak up, it is all for naught. Nothing is attempted without self-assurance.

The most important differentiators in life are being undaunted, unflappable, and broadly adequate, meaning that you have a feeling of self-worth, self-respect, self-regard, self-trust, and self-approval.

You either give an undaunted, unflappable, confident mindset to yourself, or you deprive yourself of it. Having it is the best insurance toward differentiating yourself and controlling your own destiny.

You can give this to others only if you start by giving it to yourself. That concept is important to grasp: self-confidence is not just about what it can do for you alone. It's also about what it enables you to do for others.

You're in Control of Your Thoughts

Your mind manages all of your life: your outlook, how you approach situations, and how you interact and work with others. It's a feeling of great freedom to think what you want. Sure, there are random thoughts that come and go that you can't do anything about. But the ones you put in and hold, you control.

Outside of having brain damage, disease, or mind-altering substances, you're in complete control of what goes on inside your head—if you choose to be.

You already know this, but I'm emphasizing these facts because I want you to understand how empowering they can truly be. You rule your world and run your life with the perspective you choose. Or, as one CEO told me, "Your mind is your boss, and you gotta be self-employed."

It's nearly impossible to be happy and effective at work or at home without feeling broadly adequate—that is, self-confident. This confidence triggers how you act in the world, the way you relate to everybody, and the way people relate to you.

With it you can change your mind; make decisions; delegate sooner; and have better coping methods to go over, under, around, or through problems. It also helps you to avoid a constant seeking for approval. You will trust your intuition; have a sense of peace and comfort in yourself; handle stress better; add joy to your life; give yourself freedom from needing to defer; and create better, more fulfilling lives for your children and you. And you will be more fun, interesting, intriguing, and inviting to be around.

Business befriends the self-contained. Companies would rather have a self-assured individual than a smart individual, alone. No one is more difficult to work with than an insecure person, someone you have to coddle, hand-hold, and walk on eggshells around.

The person with confidence is the person we turn to when problems of any kind arise. One of the chiefs I interviewed put it this way: "The CEO weapon of choice is a display of self-confidence."

In the business press, confident-appearing CEOs are written about with descriptions like these:

- "He spoke with such tremendous confidence and certainty, as if he'd seen, understood, and known everything from the beginning."
- "She is an island of dignified calm; . . . looks like suppressed power."
- "He was a man with a made-up mind."
- "She is extroverted without being self-aggrandizing; clearly comfortable in her own skin and intellect."

- "He is confident, though not cocky; intelligent, but not conceited; . . . a calm, easy manner; . . . a leader for our age because he delivers outstanding results without seeking fame."
- "He is a distinctly new creature: the CEO who is celebrated for being uncelebrated; . . . while he shuns self-promotion, he's charismatic."
- "He is a still person even in motion; . . . he walks as if he has all the time in the world yet still manages to cover ground quickly."
- "He has a certain understanding of self and doesn't try to put on airs. You can sit down and have a conversation with him, and he doesn't try to impress you. He has a curiosity to learn and to explain and not think a lot about himself."
- "He is not in it for his ego. He's actually in it to do good."

And then there are the ones described this way: "A veritable cocktail of success and insecurity."

My experience in being around successful executives has been this: the higher the quality of confidence, the better the manager. People don't want iffy, wimpy people to follow. As one executive put it, "You have to be rooted in self-trust in order to influence others. If you don't have it in you, you'll likely not have it in others."

Developing More Confidence

So how do you become more confident? Get a head start by dedicating yourself to confidence. Even talk to yourself if it helps! Various experts add: being in good health, regularly exercising and taking care of your body, frequently participating in activities that are fun and not just working all the time, having some close confident friends that you can trust, and being happy in your single or married status.

Frankly, money gives you confidence, too, from the sense of security it provides. Still, I know plenty of wealthy people who run scared. The National Association of Realtors will tell you that owning a home increases self-confidence. (Oh, and alcohol gives a form of it, too, as noted and celebrated in many country-and-western songs.)

Having fulfilling and enjoyable work is a confidence builder. But it's important that your attitude toward yourself not be tied strictly to your job position and title because if you lose the job, you'll likely lose your self-confidence. One CEO told me about being on top of the world on Monday, getting fired on Tuesday, and by Wednesday feeling like a failure.

But back to the self-talk: the simplest, most honest, strongest mental verbiage that you can give yourself is to expect and assume acceptance of who and what you are. Oust your harmful internal critic. You are not below or above anyone's station. Between the Creator and the Constitution, you are equal to anyone. What you do with yourself with those facts is up to you.

Regardless of your past, going forward, expect to be accepted. That means to count on and assume a favorable reception from others. The alternative is to count on, assume, and expect an *un*favorable one. Whichever you choose, you'll likely get it: a self-fulfilling prediction of self-imposed equality—or self-imposed *in*equality. The easiest thing in the world is to expect a negative response, dismissal, or rejection. With that approach, you are your first and strongest opponent. If you don't expect to be accepted, no one will accept you. If you do expect it, you just might get it.

Talk to yourself as a kind friend, not as a foe. All day long if you aren't talking to someone else, you're talking to yourself, and a lot of the time, it's destructive self-talk of being unworthy and unvalued: "I'm not good at giving speeches." "I hate small talk." "I'm bored in meetings." "I can't seem to lose this weight." "I'm always late." "I'm overwhelmed." "I'm_____ [negative this and that]." First, if someone said any of those things about you, you'd be royally miffed. Second, none of them is true. You aren't any of those things you say to yourself *all* of the time. Sometimes, yes, but it isn't you *all* the time. Third, and most significantly, it isn't the you that you want to be.

I'm all for recognizing the need for personal and professional development, but instead of telling yourself what you *aren't*, tell yourself what you want to be and what you're going to do: "I'm getting more comfortable at giving speeches." "I can hold my own in small talk conversations." "I'm getting more out of meetings lately." "I'm getting the weight under control." "I'm late less often." "I'm getting more in charge of my life."

Your brain believes what you tell it, and if you take a negative perspective, your brain supports it. If you take a positive, productive, constructive perspective, your brain supports that instead. That is true of your perspective toward yourself as well as toward others.

The self-talk that supports assuming acceptance is this: "I'm enough, I'm sufficient, I'm adequate—that is, broadly adequate." Look, you are either enough or *not* enough; sufficient or *in*sufficient; adequate or *in*adequate. And the more often and firmly you tell yourself, the more you make it so. I'm not promoting delusional self-talk of "I am great. I am wonderful." Rather, I advocate the good self-hypnosis where you remind yourself, "I'm adequate now while working to get better."

Now, just because you expect to be accepted doesn't mean you will always get a positive reception. The first reason is that the people you are dealing with may feel inadequate themselves, and they may be putting that insecurity onto you with a demonstration of false bravado, overconfidence, arrogance, or bullying. The second reason is that the people you are dealing with actually want to help you grow and be stronger. They are testing or challenging you so you can prove yourself. They know that from strife, stress, and stretching, you will grow.

Regardless of the reason, your response is what matters. You continue to assume acceptance of who you are and what you bring to the table. You'll show the people with the first reason that you won't succumb to their insecurities, and you'll prove to the second group that you are up to their challenge.

To help with confidence development, simply try "acting confident" to the outside world, practicing how it feels. The outside "show" helps the inside "take." It's okay to display confidence you don't feel, to take a leap of faith. Pretending is not faking or hiding weaknesses. It's playing the part you want to achieve.

When I coach politicians, I tell them to start behaving now as if they had already won the election. If they act the part they are seeking before they get it, it will give them practice in living this success, and it will cause voters to see them in the role, which will make the election more likely to go in their favor.

Sometimes people take offense about "acting the part," as if doing so means that they are fakes. Anyone who has children knows parenting is a fake-it-till-you-make-it experience. Surely confidence deserves the same pass. Comparable fake-it-till-you-make-it action is also what most enterprises are built on. (By the way, a good time to start your acting is first thing in the morning before your brain figures out what you're doing. Be determined to go through your day feeling undaunted. If at the beginning, the middle, or at the end of the day, you appear scared and timid, you will decrease others' confidence in you at home and in the office.)

One CEO told me, "I still doubt myself every single day. I've had painful situations, times when it was really tough. What people believe is my self-confidence is actually my acting in reaction to fear."

When you decide to be determined, then turn up the juice. Go further, and get into your *un*comfort zone. Every success story starts with someone going against popular practice or thinking. Plant a stake in the ground on some position even if it's not the most popular. If it turns out well, great. If it doesn't, you'll still have shown conviction. Do the scary. Face fears. Bad things that might possibly happen are worse in your head than in actuality. Failure will not kill you. It may make you sick for a while, but that is often your own doing in your head too.

Pros, those people who not only get promoted but also set themselves apart from amateurs, experience many setbacks, and the world does not end. You'll get more courage when you do the daunting, which helps you do the next terrifying thing. Keep at this. You will gradually experience progressive desensitization to the uncomfortable.

You will grow into your confidence just as you grow into your title, role, or even a suit of clothes. No one starts at the end point. You start somewhere, and then you make believe with new confidence, you have thoughts, feelings, and actions that you'll get there, and you let no one stop you. In time, you will get where you want to be.

At any level in any organization, there is a combination of self-satisfaction and self-doubt going on inside your head whether it's about the size of your office, cut of your clothes, who is trying to grab control over you, who is rising alongside you, and maybe who will leave you behind. There are times when you aren't smart enough, good enough, young enough, pretty enough, thin enough, or rich enough, but you have to rein in your insecurities with your mantra "I'm adequate," and then you have to go and do something above and beyond what you thought you could do or that others are afraid to try.

One CEO told me the story of being in a New York City, Park Avenue, penthouse along with 14 Fortune 50 CEOs. At one time or another, each person in the room had been on the cover of the *New York Times, Fortune, Forbes,* or the *Wall Street Journal.* All of them had been invited to this exclusive private briefing with the secretary of state to get a report on global affairs directly from the president.

The CEO told me this:

> If you want to see insecurity, put a bunch of extraordinary people next to each other. Some were as silent in their contribution as a teenage boy asking a girl for a date. No one wanted to speak up and sound dumb. They sized each other up like men do, deciding who's one-up or one-down. The evening was ending, and I made a joke about the president whereupon the other CEOs nervously glanced toward the secretary to decide on their own reaction based on hers. She burst out laughing, walked over to me, and put her arm around my shoulder in a show of camaraderie as we walked to the private elevator. . . . Sure, it made me feel good. It never hurts to intimidate the competition.

So put on the show of confidence both on the inside and the outside. Stay as cool as possible regardless of the situation.

Many people that you deal with hope for insecurity or weakness on your part because it will make it easier to manipulate you or run roughshod over you. It will also make them feel better about their own insecurities. They do not practice the art of giving acceptance even when you assume it. So you have to:

- Continue to expect it and treat them as if they are giving it to you.
- Give it to others—even more than they deserve.

Remember this: people do not wake up, look in the mirror, and say, "How can I get to [insert your name here]." Their personal protection mechanism is to wake up, look in the mirror, and say, "How do I protect myself and mine today? If it hurts [insert your name here], so be it." Most people aren't out to get you. They are trying to look after themselves since we all see ourselves at the center of the universe. Your chore is not to judge their protection approach nor let it affect your own self-talk, perspective, and behavior.

Frankly, the biggest troublemaker you'll probably have to deal with watches you shave your face or put on lipstick in your own mirror every morning.

People aren't perfect: pride, ego, arrogance, and ignorance make it so. One aspect of your self-talk (or talking to yourself) for your own sanity is to have amnesia about affronts toward you. Be indifferent to slights. Of course, you'll have to put up with intolerant coworkers at times, but then again every night you share your bed with mites, bacteria, and fungi—keep that in mind, and you can handle it!

One CEO told me that when he was a young manager, he had a difficult boss so he wrote the word "tolerance" on a piece of paper, and he has kept it in his wallet for the last 30 years. Another thing he does: "When someone is bugging me, I put some water in my mouth, don't swallow it, just swish it around until the person leaves or I calm down. It's not that the water is magic, but it causes me to keep my mouth shut." (And yes, CEOs do these things!)

Everyone has to pretend confidence. Here's one of the many times I have had to fake some of my own . . .

I was in a city's finest downtown hotel finishing preparation for a training program I was running. Nametags were laid out, gift bags in place, and the printer had completed the program with almost no mistakes. The parking lot was filling with attendees lugging bags into the lobby for the upcoming two-day stay.

The front desk manager approached me from behind and in a squeaky-scared voice hissed, "The general manager needs to have you come into his office right now. I've been told to bring you there *now*."

A little perturbed that this demand was interrupting my organizing the welcome table, but sensing that I had better do this, I asked my assistant to finish up with the gift bags and registration forms.

We walked into the manager's office, and mysteriously my escort quickly disappeared leaving me alone and looking at a grim-faced older man. Still not worried, I sat down and asked what I could do for him. I had paid the deposit stipulated in the negotiated contract, and I was fully expecting congratulations on the success of the event—"we're pleased to host you, happy you selected us, is there anything I can do for you," type of conversation.

Instead, I got this: "I've been out of the hotel on sabbatical, and generally I do not interfere with my sales department commitments, but I've just been made aware that this event is taking place. If I had known this, I would never have allowed you to come to our hotel."

I was stunned, having never been addressed like this in all the seminars I've been a part of literally around the world.

He continued, "We had a training session last quarter, and not only did they not pay their bill but they also skipped town, taking with them some hotel furnishings. While here, they brought in outside food, which was against the contract. If I remember correctly, it was buckets of KFC. The bedspreads became napkins, chicken bones stopped up the plumbing, and trash was literally dumped in the hallways. It was a very sour experience, and I won't let that happen again. So I'm prohibiting you from being here. People will be turned away at the front desk with the explanation that the program is an unethical organization."

I'd never been sucker-punched before, but I imagined this is how it would feel.

All I could come up with was, "We've been working on this for six months. We have over 200 participants. You've cashed our deposit check, and we even have the governor coming to open the event."

"I don't care. You're out of here."

"We have a signed contract."

"I don't care. And I'm not returning your money. You can sue me."

"Do you want me to explain this to the governor? I don't think he'll take too kindly to this threat."

"Go ahead."

What could I do? He was kicking me out and barring me from running my show. I could not reason with him at all. I faced financial disaster, humiliation, and a few hundred disappointed—no, mad—attendees.

In silence I looked over his shoulder, around the room, and out the window. I could see some participants approaching the lobby as we sat there. Then a force came into my body that I had not prepared for but thankfully it showed up.

I moved toward the edge of the chair, put one hand firmly on his desk, looked at him with what could be expressed as an "eye war," and spoke clearly, firmly, unequivocally, and with the slightest smile on my face: "I did not know about your bad experience, and I can imagine your anger toward such organizers. That was not me. I do not do business that way. I am going to conduct this program the next two days as agreed upon, contracted for, and planned. You can have your staff watching every step we make, but I will not stand for a hint of interruption to the event planned. Nor will I tolerate any participant's being contacted by you. If I sense, hear, or see a hint of disruption, I will immediately call the police and bring the full force of the law down on you. I'm thinking the governor would prefer not being a part of all of that. And I do not care that you are the hometown boy and I am from out of town. You, your staff, me, and my staff will fulfill our respective obligations. I will pay you for the agreed-upon costs in full when I check out. You need not find me, follow me, and invoice me. You do your part; I'll do mine. That is how this is going to be. Now, I am going back to my work. People are checking in. I expect no deviation from this plan."

Then I got up slowly (so he could take in every inch of my conviction), walked around behind his desk where he sat silent and stunned. Frankly, he was so taken aback he couldn't come up with anything to say. Once behind his desk, I reached toward his hand and shook it firmly, holding on longer than I wanted to. I put my other hand on his shoulder with a slight grip. I then stepped back, walked toward the door. I paused, turned back toward him, and added, "You and I will ensure that this program reflects well on both of us." I kept a small smile on my face while I walked out past the assistant who was nervously waiting outside but wouldn't look up at me when I walked by. "Your general manager and I have an understanding, and I expect it to be honored"—again, with the easy smile and rather piercing eye contact.

By the time I hit the elevator, I was myself again, and I couldn't believe the words that had come out of me, or the conviction and confidence I had felt and displayed to a person who had held the power in that situation.

The program went on without a hitch, and it was deemed completely successful. The participants were all happy. It was as if the confrontation had never happened.

When I checked out, I had a check made out to pay the bill in full. I envisioned the general manager's meeting me at the desk and barring my departure, maybe with backup security to ensure the payment. I steeled myself to prepare for the public encounter, but he wasn't there. The front desk manager insisted he could not accept the payment because that wasn't policy and he wouldn't know how to handle it. I said, call the general manager. He did, and when he hung up the phone, he told me this: "The general manager said have a good trip home. We will invoice you as is our custom. We look forward to hosting the program again next year."

"Fat chance," is all I thought as I left with a deep smile.

An unflappable, undaunted mindset is a mental muscle you develop. You have to keep at it, or it will atrophy. It's similar to when you break a bone: the muscles start to weaken within a week, and it can take months to rebuild them. Whether a mental muscle or physical one, it takes a lot more time to restore its strength than it takes to lose it.

Confidence Buzzkills

While you and I strive for more self-confidence, the truth is that at times we will experience situational insecurity. People, activities, and conditions will sometimes knock us off balance, at least temporarily.

All the while you are trying to maintain your self-confidence, one or many of these things will happen: a job loss, lengthy unemployment, debt, illness, relationship breakup, a competitor's achievements, a mistake in judgment, criticism, work setbacks, thinking negative thoughts about yourself, presuming others are thinking negative thoughts about you, imagining people are going against you, seeking approval from others to feel good about yourself, feeling insecure in your relationship status, or being addicted to something such as drugs, alcohol, food, or sex. Any of these occurrences will put dings in your belief system.

Accept occasional self-doubt from real or imagined setbacks as they occur; the ebb and flow are perfectly normal. It doesn't mean you are losing your confidence.

I have a slim-figured friend. I asked her how she stays that way. She said that when she's at a meal and she's considering eating more, she brings to mind how she will feel "uncomfortable and icky" if she overeats. Thinking about how badly she will feel causes her to refrain. You can do the same when you start to shrink and your confidence begins to fall. Think about how badly you will feel later, how embarrassed and mad at yourself you will be, when you behave timidly now.

When your confidence takes a hit, *do not*:

- Wake up in the morning and feel there is nothing to look forward to.
- Feel helpless, powerless, cursed, useless, unloved, unneeded, or unwanted.
- Become unmotivated and empty, asking, "What's the use?"
- Replay the negative video over and over and over in your head.
- Hold back on forgiveness for yourself or someone else.
- Feel that circumstances have gone beyond your ability to control.
- Tell yourself that you are a failure.

Instead, follow these steps:

First, don't panic and make any rash decisions leading to negative outcomes; if you do, that will only create more insecurity.

Then spend some time alone—not moping around but just being quiet in a distraction-free and electronic-free place that relaxes you and gets you away from the fray. Be kind to yourself. Remember that it's acceptable to feel badly once in a while. One or two days out of a few months is tolerable. Breathe, stretch, exercise, and regroup. Tell yourself, "This is what I trained my brain for."

Objectively review the mortifying situation. Briefly and one time only, write down what led up to it—the decisions, actions, and outcomes.

Once written down and saved for personal documentation, shake that version out of your mind, and replace it with what could have happened. Try out other confidence-displaying versions. And every time the bad memory slips into your consciousness, shake up the visual in your head again. Keep at it. Do not replay the original negative situation because you're playing only one side of a multidimensional situation. If it slips in, pinch yourself and go back to the new thoughts.

Review the things you've done well: problems solved, good decisions made, bad situations you've overcome, and accomplishments to date. Don't undervalue what you've done.

Pick something you do well, and go do it! Get some confidence restored by even a small accomplishment. If possible, pick something related to your setback, not something random. After the hotel general manager had challenged the ethics of people who were in the training business, that weekend I delivered some of the best speeches I've ever given.

Remind yourself that even if you made a worthless decision, you aren't a worthless person.

The ultimate confidence builder is realizing that after being knocked down, you were able to rebuild a situation, and you can do it again when necessary.

Save being scared for something really worth it.

Overconfidence

Please note: I'm for overall confidence, which is quite different from overconfidence—or arrogance, meaning a swollen ego with indifference to others. Overconfidence is an inferiority complex that is mistakenly labeled a "superiority complex."

People whose low self-esteem, insecurities, and fears are revealed with a conceited cockiness, a know-it-all attitude, an inflated ego, a power trip, self-absorption, narcissism, and hubris are big problems in management. You can't judge them. You can only marvel at the conceit and the smugness that make them so blind to their behavior.

The confident person would say, "If you want the answer, come to me." The arrogant one would say, "Who do you think you are, talking to me that way?" Or as more than one actor on video has been caught saying to an arresting officer, "Do you *know* who I am?"

Acting aggressively and being overbearing, superior, rude, or arrogant have nothing to do with self-confidence and everything to do with insecurities. Such behaviors are self-protective offense and defense mechanisms that people use to guard and assuage their own ego, to hide their shyness, and to keep you from seeing how un-self-confident they are. If you delve into the source of their behavior, you will find that it most likely stems from:

- Personal discontent and heavy self-criticism.
- Hostility toward others in general and irritability without cause.
- Hypersensitivity to disapproval and an excessive wish to please.
- Feeling attacked and/or victimized; envy, invidiousness, and resentment.
- Chronic indecisiveness; striving for impossible perfection.
- Dwelling on past mistakes; fear of making more mistakes.
- Seeing the downside first, foremost, and for the foreseeable future.
- Clinging to negative, pessimistic, self-defeating thoughts without cause.
- Chronic laziness and procrastination.

Unless you live in their head, you can't fully understand how weak their confidence is or where their lack of confidence stems from. You almost have to sympathize with them because it can be truly tiring for them to have to work so hard at pretending they do not feel insecure.

If you catch yourself crossing the line into caustic behavior, stop, consider the source of it, and change your behavior before you do damage to yourself or others.

Frankly, I am less concerned that you will be overconfident than I am concerned that you will not experience the self-confidence that you deserve.

Reacquainting Yourself with You

The best confidence builder is to truly know yourself. It's your ongoing, lifelong duty: to acquire self-knowledge. It's not so much to find yourself though, as it is to create yourself. Just as you can choose to think whatever you want, you can choose to be whomever you want.

It takes serious thought, self-examination, and reflection to find out whom you are at this point so you can decide whom you want to be going forward. Mike Barkley, vice president of Campbell's Soup, said it well:

> I think knowing yourself is a vastly underrated skill. Part of knowing yourself is not letting others—people, companies, or even society—impose their viewpoints or will on yours. Someone once told me, "Don't let people should all over you—you should do this or you should do that." . . . advice easier given than heeded sometimes, but wise all the same.

There are reportedly over 2,500 different personality tests on the market, but I'm less interested in your taking one of them than I am in your writing down your life story. Why? Who you are comes from your exposure to date—a sum of all your experiences—and it's beneficial to ponder about it. So write your story.

The purpose of writing your story is not to navel-gaze but to take a personal inventory, make a self-assessment, inspect your life, and "peel back the onion a little." It is also to help you:

- Find your own truth to grasp what makes you, you.
- Know where your instincts come from and find all sides of your nature.
- Get knowledge of your character and feelings, and find the emotional biases and beliefs you carry around.
- Make yourself aware of things simmering below the surface so you can understand your anxieties.
- Identify your strengths and capabilities so you can leverage them as you need to.
- Isolate your weaknesses, know your blind spots, and identify your limitations to overcome. (One CEO told me, "I'd rather be made aware of my failings through self-reflection than from friends.")
- Get a handle on all of your hard and soft assets.
- Accurately assess your talents and see what makes you special—what makes you one of one.
- See what you're really committed to.
- Realize what and how your kids learned from you.
- Communicate well and share your background clearly, effectively, and thoroughly.
- Define your personal brand.

As one business guru told me, "When you know yourself, you know others."

When my friend Dan Munroe decided to go to law school, he sized up his chances as slim: Bs, not As, and not high LSAT scores. But he applied, and he went for an interview at the school of his choice even though he didn't think he had a shot. While in his hotel room the night before, he got the idea to make a list of how he was different from other people—a list of attributes that made him unique. The next day at the interview, he was asked if he had anything to say to the selection committee. He said, "I'd like to tell you why I'd be a good student here," and he then elaborated on the strengths and positive differences he'd written down the night before. To everyone's surprise, including his, he got in (only 1 applicant in 200 make it). At graduation, the dean made a point to come up to Dan to personally congratulate him, saying, "You know, you were in the decline pile, but when you came up with your list of why you're different, we changed our mind."

Hal Johnson, chairman of human resources for Korn/Ferry International, told me this:

> When looking at comparably competent people, the biggest differentiator is actual, describable, verifiable accomplishment. How did something change because this individual did something specific about it? How did the person make lemonade out of the lemons he was given . . . and how did he do it, with a boss, peers, and subordinates . . . and then be able to describe what he actually accomplished? Sounds easy, but most can't.

Start writing your own story on your next long flight or bad weather weekend. Better yet, don't wait for either of those. Just start today. Yes, today! Right now, grab a sheet of paper and file folder (electronic or paper), and start putting down notes about past and present work accomplishments and anecdotal memories that pop into your head— favorite family stories, the facts, dates, and time frames of major events, and so on. Write about:

- Where you were born and under what circumstances.
- What kind of work your parents did in your formative years, and then later on into your teen years.
- Your home life and relationships as a child, and then later as you grew into a young adult.
- The successes and setbacks you experienced in grade school, high school, and college.
- The people in your family today and your relationships with siblings and friends.
- The experiences that shaped or changed your life—personally and professionally.

- Why you chose your first company; why you left it.
- Why you chose the next company. Continue up to where you are now and why.
- What your bosses and your mentors taught you.
- Your losses and wins at work.
- The shining moments in your life.
- What you do for fun.
- What skills and talents you have now and then the ones you want to work on. (Include the soft skills of tactfulness, savvy, and calmness.)
- Your personal philosophy toward life, and your personal motto.
- The biggest surprise you've discovered in life.
- The best advice you've received.
- Your biggest regrets: what do you wish you'd done differently?
- What you still want to do in life—both personally and professionally.

Use a simple outline to organize your story. You'll want to include many anecdotes. You'll need to first set the anecdote scene and the situation. Next, you'll explain what you did about it, particularly as compared to what others were doing about it. And finally, what resulted? What happened?

Keep it as a living document and a personal chronicle. Add to it as you encounter new experiences, adventures, successes, and even setbacks.

WRITE YOUR STORY

Write an abridged story today—that is, right now—by filling in these blanks:

- When I was in my teens, I wanted to be _____
- But I'm glad that I became _____
- If I weren't in my current occupation, I'd be _____
- If I could rewrite my history, the three things I'd change are _____

- The most surprising thing I've learned about myself _____
- I've learned to appreciate my_____
- When I need motivation, I _____
- The best compliment I've received is _____
- My proudest moment was _____
- The worst day of my life was _____
- Most people don't know that I _____
- The way I'd like to be remembered is _____

I can unequivocally guarantee you that there is no one else in the entire world who can tell the exact same story that you can—and that's part of finding your uniqueness (and self-confidence).

When Jack Falvey, CEO of MakingTheNumbers.com and frequent *Wall Street Journal* columnist, performed this exercise and wrote his life story, he ended up with 175,000 words. To put that in perspective, this book is around 60,000. Jack shared his document with me, and it was was titled "Volume I," and he said he had Volumes II and III yet to write.

Another CEO told me, "Writing my story reminded me of my unique self, which comes from Northwestern, Harvard, IBM, and the pimps I grew up with."

Recruiters like to proclaim that your past is a predictor of your future. I argue with that sentiment because there are parts of everyone's past that can't be changed and aren't their faults. Still, you always need to appreciate your starting point to determine where you want to go. Writing it down puts it front and center in your consciousness.

Whatever you have experienced is where you have *been*, not where you are going. As a thinking adult, it's your choice as to how you plan to live going forward. Regardless of how you were raised or taught by your mom and dad, you have a right to choose your destiny—and that builds confidence on its own.

One CEO told me that in his retirement he went back through his business life story and decided it would make a good novel, so he's writing it now. He said, "It's about using a legitimate electronics company to launder very large sums of money for organized crime organizations. It is fiction, but was based on a true story where I was a whistle blower."

More than one CEO told me some version of adding to their life story when they go on business trips in the form of a letter to their children. As one explained: "It keeps me close to them in my mind since I travel so much. . . . I don't send the letters, as they are too young to appreciate them. I just collect them and add them to my file with the hope that some day the letters will benefit them in their own life. Sometime later I'll bind the document and give it as a gift to my children"—which it truly is. Think about it, wouldn't it be interesting to know all that about your own parents? If they are alive, ask them before it's too late to learn the answers.

Better yet, get them to write their story. One of my most treasured items is my mom's writing about her life as a little girl, her dreams, her desire to "make $1,000 of her own someday," her first job teaching at a county school, all the way to her successful sales career earning international achievement awards and being pictured in *Time* magazine.

NOTE TO WORKING PARENTS

A special note to all you working parents reading this book who sometimes feel guilty about being away from home. I'm the product of a dual-career couple, and every bit of their both working full time helped me, not harmed me, in my childhood and through my formative years. By their example, my parents taught me how to make a living and also how to live. I'm the third generation of working women in my family. A favorite photograph in my office is of my grandmother standing knee deep in a mountain of milo that my grandfather and she had harvested on their family farm. So parents, don't feel the guilt. Instead, feel the pride in the lessons you're teaching your children.

Just today, a seasoned (a nice way of saying "old") CEO told me, "I took the weekend to write down what I'm good at. It was pretty interesting, and I shared it with my wife so she could be impressed too!" I thought that was pretty cool that in the winter of his career he still found it beneficial to add to his story.

Here are some situations that came out of my conversations with CEOs who told about how their early experiences shaped them. You can use these experiences as prompts for your own story writing:

- "At six years old I got up at 4 a.m. to beat the heat as I mowed and maintained our three-acre yard in Connecticut. I did such a good job that the neighboring nuns from a convent would walk by and praise me. Later on, the CEO of the company I worked for shared his story of mowing lawns at a young age. I told him I did too. Because of this common experience, he got to know me even though I was very junior, and he took me on as a mentee."

- "My dad headed public works in our city, and I figured he'd get me a cushy well-paying job my freshman year of college— 'Consider it done' was his response when I asked. He did get me a job as a trash man who hung on the back of the truck as I emptied cans into the maggot-filled bucket and other stinky things. It certainly made me see what really hard work was."

- "I was rather disruptive in high school, and some football buddies and I would bring food to the class, crack jokes, and just generally mess around. The teacher took me aside and said, 'I'll make you a deal. You don't come to class, and I'll give you an A.' I didn't, and she did. It was my senior year, and I ended up skipping so many classes that I had to leave all of my stuff in my locker at graduation because I couldn't remember the combination since I'd never opened it."

- "My high school coach took me aside one day and said, 'You're from a good family, and you have it made. Your teammate over there has only one shot in life so I'm going to make him first string, not you.' It made me mad. I had words with the coach, and I quit. But now running a company, I see why he did it."

- "I became a lawyer because my father hated lawyers more than anything else."
- "I grew up in a white community, and my dad always told me in order to be equal, you have to be better. Speaking, diction, academic, physical, and moral behavior had to be excellent. He'd say, 'They won't allow you to go through the lunch line twice. . . . Never do anything half-measure; pursue hard and with complete dedication.'"

These are a few pages from my own story that helped me understand myself.

My parents didn't believe in babysitters, which wasn't that unusual in the early 1950s. My brother was four years older than I was, and they figured there was enough age difference for him to be responsible for me. That meant I ended up doing what he wanted to do, and what he wanted to do was to hunt and fish.

I remember one particular day when he was 10 and I was 6 that I was walking behind him with a dead, stiff jack rabbit clutched in my small, cold hands. He had instructed me to gingerly move from soft tuft of field grass to soft tuft; I was careful not to step on a stick for fear of making any unwanted noise.

My brother could spot animal tracks in the soft dirt and patches of snow and tell me in which direction the animal had gone and how long ago. He knew what bush and weed would camouflage two big rabbit ears. He pointed out the rabbits' sunning place, the clump of fur caught on a thistle, and how the rabbit scat differed from that of other little critters. He was patient. And he taught me what he knew as he showed me the circular pattern the rabbit would run when alarmed and the spot it would likely return to. So we stood in a crouched position and waited. And my brother was right. The rabbit did return, attempting to hide itself with its ears laid back flush against its body. But the rabbit's eye could not be hidden, and my brother took careful, quiet aim and felled supper for my family. With another rabbit in hand, together we trekked on to our next prey.

For my brother and me to be given this much freedom by my parents, we had to live up to what we'd been taught about our personal responsibility. My little six-year-old mind told me this is a good situation to be in, and I wanted more of it.

My parents' children were everything that was important to them. They genuinely liked us, and they trusted us. That is something children understand, and my brother and I tried to live up to their positive expectations.

On that cool fall day in a Kansas farm field, I resolved to write a book on "how to hunt with your brother." I was just starting to read books, but something in me said to write one. I guess that I figured everyone would want to know what I was being taught. I couldn't put words to it then, but now I understand it as self-reliance and self-confidence.

Well, I never wrote that book, specifically, but if you look at the how-to nature of what I teach in doing whatever you are doing, better, I guess you could say I'm writing a variation on such a book now!

And then this story from 40 years later . . .

Sometime back I was speaking to a group of 300 technology CEOs in Tucson, Arizona. Everyone in the audience, at least on paper, was a kazillionaire. I'm not a kazillionaire, and frankly I was feeling a bit intimidated by the powerhouse audience. So I phoned home for a little pep talk, explaining my trepidation. My husband's advice to me was, "Just slow down. You know your expertise. They hired you to share it, so go and do it." Then I called my parents, still feeling some unease. My mom's suggestion was, "Say a prayer." Then my dad got on the phone and gave his guidance: "Give 'em hell, turn it on, get right to it, tear into them, and straighten them out."

As you know, we are a sum of our experiences.

What matters most to you, says the most about you.

When you reflect on your past and see what you've done in life, given what you were given, you can feel pretty good about yourself. And then, when you make something out of it larger than yourself, that's the ultimate confidence builder.

Confidence is your friend; insecurity is your foe.

CHAPTER 2

Be Trusted

Pᴇʀʜᴀᴘs ᴛʜᴇ word I have heard most often from CEO and C-level executives as to what gets their positive attention is "trust":

- "I want someone I can trust."
- "The person needs to be trustworthy."
- "I've got to be able to put trust in the individual to know I can count on him or her."
- "People have to be able to trust him to pat them on the back."
- "She needs to show me a pattern of trust that is predictable and reliable."
- "She's got to be trusted not to be mediocre."
- "He's got to be trusted not to steal."

When I've asked them to explain further the concept of trust, they've told me that it's when you:

- "Treat the company money as your own."
- "Say what you'll do, then do it."
- "Are conscientious."
- "Keep your honor clean."
- "Don't subscribe to 'If no one knows, it didn't happen.'"
- "Show impeccable character in how you treat your associates, how you handle your expense reports, how you follow up and do what you've promised, and how you keep your word."

Although *trust* can be a little murky to define, when CEOs discuss the topic, they're talking about integrity, honesty, morality, principles, ethical behavior, character, and being upright. Now those attributes might seem odd, since "chiefs" of all types are often the people being pointed out as lacking such qualities.

It's true that not all business leaders are pillars of perfection—some CEOs and C-level executives are liars, cheats, and lechers. But sometimes they are producing the numbers that stockholders want to see, and so they keep their job. (Please note that I carefully chose the people I interviewed for this book, and they are the good ones as opposed to the not-so-good ones.)

Whether you have a straight-shooting CEO and/or manager or not, I can assure you of this:

- If you slip up even once in maintaining your integrity on the job, you'll have to put in double and triple efforts to *try* to recover management's trust.
- Once trust is broken, you won't necessarily get fired, but you'll almost never be trusted completely again.
- You'll no longer be groomed or primed for advancement.

As it was put to me, "In a job you are either tutored for development, or you are used for what they can get out of you. Even if you are off-the-charts brilliant, [if you lose their trust], you will be just an exotic menial."

Why is being trusted a big differentiator? There are two main reasons. First, people don't generally trust "businesspeople." A 2012 Gallup poll found that only 21 percent of survey respondents trusted business executives to be honest and ethical. Since around 2000, ratings have dropped with regard to trust for numerous other professionals, including bankers, accountants, building contractors, daycare providers, college teachers, and clergy. If you are trustworthy, you immediately stand out in the population. The second reason being trusted is a major differentiator is that it is a quality that results in letting your boss relax with you. Employers know that almost all employees lie, steal, or cheat to some degree (it may be as minor as lifting a felt-tip pen or as major as padding expense accounts or engaging in fraud). As one CEO said, "You are going to get ripped off or swiped from unless you are a Ma and Pa operation and *you* are the Ma and Pa."

If your boss trusts you and she does not need to be "on guard" about your behavior, you'll stand out positively.

If you fall into the majority of people who are considered untrustworthy, others won't want to do business with you, and you will propagate negative behavior in your subordinates.

None of this positive behavior, however, requires four years in the ministry or close study of the Bible, Torah, or Qur'ān. It does require returning a phone call when you said you would; sending the book you offered to loan when you said you would; getting to the 2 p.m. appointment by 2 p.m. if you agreed to be there; following up the way you guaranteed you would; and completing the report when you promised you would. I understand that things change, crises pop up, and you can't always do what you said you would do, or do it when and how you said you would. But as soon as you know that you can't, contact the people involved and explain the situation: "I told you I'd be there at 2 p.m., but it's going to be 3:30. If that is not convenient for you, let's reschedule a time that works for you. In the meantime I will e-mail the information you wanted at the 2 p.m. appointment now to help minimize your inconvenience." Or "The report is due on Friday. Today is Wednesday, and I'm going to need until Monday. I'm working straight through on it, but some problems have come up, and I need to do some more research, which means that I need a couple more days to finish it. What can I provide you now to help you out with the Friday deadline if Monday causes you a problem?"

Now, trust works both ways. You deserve the same respect you show others. But you're not always going to get it. So worry more about fulfilling your end of things and less about their not fulfilling theirs. If you don't trust your managers or whomever you work with to treat you similarly, separate yourself from the situation as soon as you realistically can. First, you don't want to learn those bad lessons and take on the habit yourself, and, second, you can't let their behavior inhibit you from doing your own good work.

You have to make choices throughout all of your life to sustain a reputation of integrity—both in whom you associate with and how you behave. One mentor told me early in my career to "plan to pay ransom for your good name." Shortly thereafter, I experienced that situation. I hired a production company to produce a promotional video, and I agreed to pay the flat fee required. Upon completion, they billed me 50 percent more than we had contracted for, explaining that it had taken more time than they had planned. All I could do was pay the extra money—that is, pay ransom for my good name. Had I not, the production company could have honestly told people, "She didn't pay her bill"—likely not adding, "Of course, we billed her 50 percent more than we contracted for."

Integrity is one of those areas where everyone feels they have it but what they actually have is their perspective of the concept. You see, the nature of integrity—like beauty, goodness, and fairness—is in the eye of the beholder, mostly due to the values instilled and the lessons taught at a young age.

Integrity and Your Frame of Reference

The main reason any discussion on integrity is squishy is that the word's definition varies for individuals based on what they were taught by their early influencers: mamas, papas, sisters, brothers, teachers, coaches, mentors, bosses, and friends.

That's where we learn our frame of reference for general behavior and specifically for what is right and wrong. Therefore, as one CEO put it, "What was done for you and what was done to you, now makes you, you."

Amateurs assume others have the same thoughts and expectations that they do; pros understand that everyone had unique influencers and upbringings, causing people to think differently from each other.

Some of these early influencers might have been renowned ethicists, politicians, ministers, a single parent holding down three jobs, a mail carrier, fire fighter, or meteorologist; they may have been caring, loving, hardworking, well-meaning people. But they also could have been abusive, neurotic, psychotic, or chronically and deeply depressed; they may have been alcoholics, liars, cheaters, addicts, and ne'er-do-wells. As one CEO told me: "The beliefs we are taught are so strong, that is what wars are fought for . . . because human beings have always found it easier to fight for their principles than to live up to them."

Experts say most of the basic makeup of your character is acquired before the age of 15. What you were taught by early influencers is likely what you are now teaching your children. How many times have you caught yourself sounding just like your parent? The problem here is that sometimes we find that we've picked up some bad habits from our influencers: negative thoughts, low self-esteem, even destructive behaviors. Some of what we were taught will end up working against us and our goals. Recognizing this fact is imperative so that we can avoid passing these limiting thoughts and behaviors down to the people we are most influencing, whether in our home or in our office. (That's another reason for you to write your story: to recall, reflect on, and better understand what your mom, dad, and other influencers taught you.) Your beliefs can be deeply embedded, but you can still choose to leave them behind. Choosing how, who, and what you are as a thinking adult is one of your freedoms.

Once again, keep in mind, however, that the people you deal with have had their own upbringing, and it has been just as significant and life shaping to them as yours has been to you. Their "right way" is correct to them, just as your "right way" is correct to you. Yours is not *more* right. So words like "trust" or "integrity" have no intrinsic meaning. Their meanings consist of the values *you* assign to them.

What your parents taught you is what it is. (Well, it's actually what their mom and dad taught them.) Maybe it's not what you need to create the standard of character that you want, so you elect to change. You can have beliefs that are deeply embedded and still choose to leave them behind. Choosing how, who, and what you are as a thinking adult is one of your freedoms.

Consider this: whether something is true or false often depends on the eye of the beholder. Memory and truth are close but not the same. The boundary between recollection and imagination can easily be crossed. People believe their memories are straightforward and reliable. They aren't. In fact, sometimes their memories are complete fabrications. "Truth is as real as it can be about events that didn't happen," said Kurt Wiese, president of Summit and former private contractor to the U.S. State Department in Afghanistan and Iraq. "It's easy to make your stories sound cooler as time goes on."

THE TRUTH ABOUT TRUTH

- Understand your truth is as you see it, just as other people's truth is how they see it.
- Tell your truth as you know it, regardless of how difficult it is. You will only complicate things if you obfuscate and deceive.
- Tell your truth even when you could get away with something by not telling it.
- Accept that not telling the truth can have unintended consequences for weeks, months, and years because people will never really know if they can trust you.
- Know that when you do tell the difficult, uncomfortable truth, you will build trust for weeks, months, and years.
- Telling it the way you see it lets you sleep better at night.
- Don't judge others' standards, but know and stick to your own.

People justify telling untruths because at the time, doing so seems more tactful and political, or it might save face, avoid accountability, minimize confrontation, make things go more smoothly, or prevent hurt feelings.

Anita Kelly, University of Notre Dame psychology professor, found that people who tell fewer falsehoods feel better mentally and physically. Maybe that explains why we need more healthcare—according to the American Psychological Association, Americans lie on average 11 times per week.

One CEO told me this story:

> Some people think omission is lying. I don't. My fiancée came to me one day and said, "Someone told me that you have an ex-wife and two children?" "Yes, I do." Awhile later she said, "Someone told me you have two ex-wives and four children." "Yes, I do," I answered. Then she accused me of lying. I said, "I never lie. I have never lied. You just never asked so I didn't bring it up."

Certainly there is congruence of honesty if there is a rule of law or if you are part of a group with an ethical code of conduct: lawyers and accountants have such a code; some companies have a code of conduct; and religions have teachings and commandants. Even gang members have a collective judgment for what is allowed, what's frowned upon, and what's downright forbidden.

Make up your mind about what integrity means for you, and stick to your beliefs. Instead of sinking to the level of questionable integrity accepted in your department, function, industry, or company, stay true to your own standard despite all pressure and how easy it would be, "just this one time" to give in.

Stick to Your Beliefs

The best you can do is to tell the truth as you see it and do what you say you'll do with bosses colleagues, customers, clients, competitors, and vendors. You will stand out because you are simply less suspect. Whatever it involves, if you stay steady to truth and commitment despite outside pressure to do otherwise, you'll create trust, and you will be a more attractive employee or leader for it.

"I just tell people the truth. If I tell the truth, I never have to remember what I told anyone," says Bill Daniels, CEO of Daniels Cablevision and cofinancier of ESPN. You don't want to be like the employee whose manager described him this way: "He used to take pride in his integrity. Now he barely remembers the word." Or the man who said this: "I don't want to lie, but I do."

Richard Toeppe, vice president of manufacturing for Fenner-Dunlop, told me this story about an occasion early in his career when a boss asked him to do something Richard thought unethical:

Upon the request, the response that went through my mind was that I needed to give myself time to think, so I said his words back to him to make sure I understood the request. He then repeated the request so I knew that I was correct in my understanding. I told him I could not make happen what he wanted to happen. He asked me why. I told him it was against what I felt was legal. He told me he didn't see it that way. We went back and forth on the issue for a while. Then I told him, "I am not doing the task, and if I lose my job standing by my values, I can live with that, but I could not live with making it happen and keeping my job." We did not take action on the task after the discussion. Later that year we were in a meeting and someone from the executive team questioned my uprightness, and my boss said he has never worked with anyone with as much integrity as I have. The boss and I are still very close, and I consider him one of the best bosses I have every worked for.

Richard's boss was able to relax, and he didn't need to worry that he or the company may get ripped off under Richard's watch. This is a huge separator where others who haven't taken such a strong stand look suspect in relation to those who have done so. The mental cost of watching an employee, keeping tabs on his or her actions, is quite high, and if this burden is lifted from the boss, you will stand out positively.

It's easier to keep true to your sense of integrity than to recover from the lack of it. And just as in the story above, when someone notices it, you are the better employee, boss, and person for it. There is no win, no advantage, no victory worth even a blemish on your own code of honor. And that is aside from the fact that nothing travels faster than a negative word about you. As one politician said, "Trust arrives on foot, but leaves in a Ferrari."

If others see that you break the contract, the code "just this once" it's all over for your reputation; you won't count. At the very least you will become suspect.

One CEO told me this story:

Early in my career I ran a hotel in Europe. I was young competing against older hoteliers—a lot of whom were ex-military officers in Europe. And I found out that so much of what goes on is bull****. These guys had learned to lie and cheat and steal to survive, and they kept up their lesson. . . . They went to church with their families on Sundays, and they were lauded in the community. To me it was a real dark side, and it made me think ambition was unsavory.

Bribery and lying are not censured in many parts of the world. One CEO told me, "I grew up in Vienna, Austria, and I know how to tell seven different kinds of lies." A South Korean executive commented to his U.S. partner, "The United States is the only country that believes somebody is telling the truth." A U.S. CEO who emigrated to Russia to work was told by his new assistant, "Never believe a word they say here; for them a lie is the truth."

People in some cultures don't want to tell you "no" so they will give you an answer that doesn't answer the question you asked. They may nod in affirmation, but they have no intention of doing what they are saying they will do. What means "yes" to some means "no" or "maybe" to others. In Arabic countries, *inshallah* means "if God is willing" or "maybe." One CEO experienced in working in that culture said this: "I would ask if I could pick up the product at the store on Friday, and the shop owner would nod his head and say '*inshallah*.' It took me a month of drinking tea with him to really make it happen."

Politicians worldwide are known to and are pretty much expected to manipulate the truth, if not outright lie. One CEO, who is also the cousin of a former U.S. president, said to me: "Only an idiot would think you can get elected without lying." Which helps to explain a former U.S. secretary of state's comment: "It's not a lie. It's a terminological inexactitude."

During an election of a new pope, I heard a cardinal say on television, "Well, to be honest with you . . . ," and I thought that should be a given. But then I've read that the world's most shoplifted book is the Bible, so go figure!

One company president told me this story about legal action he had recently settled:

> Money was missing at my company. In our business some people send cash payments to us in the mail, which the receptionist routinely opened. I called her into my office, and I explained my suspicions and questioned her. She got mad and threatened to sue for false accusation and defamation of character. Obviously things went downhill from there; her anger just increased, and the situation ended up with lawyers getting involved. Turns out her boyfriend who visited her during his lunch hour actually took the money, with her knowledge, but in her eyes she was innocent because she wasn't the thief.

Situational ethics is how the world works, according to Fritz Allhoff, a professor at Western Michigan University. He writes about "role-differentiated morality," where saying something that is false or even an out-and-out lie, fibbing, bluffing, spinning, misleading, giving B.S., deceiving, exaggerating, or omitting something or creating a strategic deception is permissible and even obligatory with certain roles. Allhoff writes this:

> A lawyer makes his client's case, a soldier kills, a CEO paints the rosiest possible picture. . . . Different perspectives and sometimes roles make for various perspectives on integrity. If a company sends out a press release announcing that the president has resigned to spend more time with his family when in fact he was fired, or if the marketing department puts out advertising reporting "customers are delighted" when they aren't, if an aging executive dyes his hair, a CEO protects company secrets—is it a lack of integrity?

In every culture, country, and company. there are people who can look you right in the eye and tell the "truth" as they see it when it is a "lie" to the listener. The fact of the matter is that the best you can do at the end of the day is tell the truth as you see it. Don't intentionally mislead or misrepresent. Don't break commitments, go back on your word, or waltz around an issue. And, as a little extra incentive, don't forget, even for a moment, that depending on the situation, you can wind up in jail for your dishonesty.

So How Do You Manage the Truth?

As a pro, find out how other people view things. There has to be some common understanding about ethics. Without that, it's a free-for-all. Then codify the agreed-upon code, meaning by writing it down, communicating it, and enforcing it.

A code not written down is not enforced.

If your boss doesn't engage in conversation with you on this concept because human resources warns her against it, you have to approach the subject. Go to your boss and ask what is expected and acceptable behavior. You need to know what her mom and dad taught her in addition to the organizational code.

And even then, remember some dos and don'ts:

- DO understand that misunderstandings happen all the time.
- DO realize that one person's honesty might be another person's dishonesty.
- DO be honest with yourself.
- DON'T intentionally mislead, misrepresent, tell half-truths, fib, or allow strategic omissions.
- DON'T go back on your word—or your word in their eyes.
- DON'T forget that people go to jail for dishonesty.

"We make mega-million-dollar deals without a contract, just a handshake. . . . I don't look at the deal. I look at the people. Good people can make a bad deal good; bad people can make a good deal bad," says Ron Arvine, founder of Arvine Pipe & Supply Company.

Spend less time judging a colleague's integrity and more time maintaining yours. It causes others to mistrust you if you question theirs.

Being a person more people trust sets you apart in hiring and promotion decisions as well as in delegating and leading. You have a better chance of positively influencing anyone around you when you know where you stand and stick to your convictions without compromising and bending to pressure. If you are honest in all your business dealings, you will be one less deceptive player in the picture, and your trustworthiness will lead to your success.

CHAPTER 3

Be Optimistic and Easy to Get Along With

THE ONLY things you can control in this world are your attitudes and your effort. You have little or no say over the craziness of your colleagues, boss, the government, or your family, but you can take charge of your own actions and how you interact with others. As a thinking adult, your outlook on life is managed by you, not by others, although they will try hard to do so. Don't let them. You are your own boss in this matter, so be a good one.

Why is this good-natured attitude a differentiator? Consider the following: in a 1957 study, 35 percent of Americans said they were happy people. According to R. Murali Krishna, MD and president of the Oklahoma State Board of Health, a similar study conducted recently showed that only 30 percent of Americans considered themselves to be happy people. In a 2013 Harris poll, one in three people expressed satisfaction with their life. And that same year, a Gallup poll found that 70 percent of employees were not "engaged" (Gallup's word for job enjoyment and satisfaction).

I've seen studies saying that anywhere from 1 to 45 percent of people enjoy their work. Those studies have also found that people at the beginning and at the end of their career are most engaged; women are slightly more engaged than men; and people with college degrees feel less engaged than those with less education.

Optimistic, good-natured people who are easy to get along with immediately differentiate themselves from the majority, especially in the workplace. I'm using these terms as a précis for liking yourself, being outgoing versus being self-oriented, being pleasant and cheerful without relying on others to give you a boost, having satisfaction and contentment in your work, and enjoying a fulfilling life.

People who are optimistic and easy to get along with will stand out because the majority of people, quite frankly, are bitter or painfully serious, feel victimized, and are quick to criticize.

Make no mistake, being easy to get along with, even being nice, is *not* a sign of weakness. The strongest, most powerful, and most influential people can afford to be affable. The insecure, the bullies, the people with a victim mindset, and the people who fake a strong bravado are the weak ones.

CEOs tell me all the time some version of the following:

- "I can easily hire qualified people, but it's not so easy to find people with a good outlook."
- "I hire attitude. Skills can be learned. I'll take good attitude any day."
- "I can teach people the technical side of the business a lot easier than I can teach them how to have a good mindset."
- "I no longer hire for technical skills. Instead, I hire mainly on personality and work ethics. Not only does technology change so often that people have to constantly learn new things but also, people who understand technology are not necessarily able to interface with customers, and they can quickly do more damage than good."
- "What catches my eye in an employee? Someone who has a positive attitude about everything, leaves problems at home, is uplifting, and turns crap into gold."
- "If I have a choice of two people who are comparably talented, I will always choose to go with the one who has the can-do, 'Hey, boss, we can get this done' attitude. Frankly, it's too tiring to have to coax and cajole a negative person."
- "I don't have a lot of patience for a person who always acts like there is a rain cloud parked over his boat."
- "I want people who calm trouble and soothe rough edges, who are even-keeled, who are happy with themselves. . . . They don't have to be jolly and joking; they just need to be more amiable than most."

If that doesn't make it clear enough, let me recap that if given a choice, the CEOs prefer to have around them an individual who:

- Has an inexhaustible good nature and is habitually affable.
- Has a determined cheerfulness and is easygoing even in adversity.
- Is happily disposed and always on an even keel.
- Is flexible and not easily rattled. Doesn't always have to have things go his or her way.
- Is always pleasant.
- Is uncomplicated, without drama.
- Does not feel like a victim.
- Continually chooses a productive, constructive perspective rather than a destructive, negative, sour, sullen, dissatisfied, agitated, and discontented viewpoint.

I had a female executive client who is African-American. In the course of our conversation, I asked her if she'd be comfortable talking about some of her experiences growing up with discrimination. She looked at me with a slight are-you-crazy expression, and she replied: "I have no idea what you are talking about. I never faced any discrimination." Then in response to my own are-you-crazy look, she smiled and added, "Well, I chose never to see it." She was being totally honest when she relayed to me how she chose to view it.

Choosing your perception of yourself, your life, and others is one of the most pure freedoms you have.

One of my students from the University of Northern Colorado (UNC) graduated and started a job in an energy company in a small Southwestern city, a place much different from where he had spent his college years. Let's just say he went from living in what people call "God's country" to a place with far fewer natural features. I asked him how he was handling the change of scenery. With sincere enthusiasm, he said, "I love it. I'm where the action is for my industry. It's exciting every single day. Oh, sure, it's not as green as where I'm from, but everything else makes up for it."

It's human nature to gravitate toward people, information, or places that imply a happier outlook. You provide that outlook for yourself, one that no one can take away. Frankly, few of us have any justification for the negative, pessimistic perspective that we let ourselves get bogged down with. No matter what you're going through that's tough, unless you're using your last breath on earth, it's not that rough or as a bad as it can seem. In fact, you can manage your own perspective about the immediate world around you, and doing so:

- Helps in any struggle.
- Costs nothing out of your pocket.
- Buys you time to think before you act.
- Causes people *not* to avoid you.
- Makes you viewed more favorably and for a longer period of time.
- Makes you appear confident and self-assured.
- Gives you a better day today and better memories when you look back on this day.

You know all of this to be true. Somewhere along the line, you were taught that "you can catch more flies with honey than you can with vinegar." We all know this, but few of us exert consistent control over this matter. The father of Taoism, Lao-Tze, wrote in 615 BC: "Watch your thoughts; they become words. Watch your words; they become actions. Watch your actions; they become habits. Watch your habits; they become characteristics. Watch your characteristics; they become your destiny." These thoughts are nothing new, yet most people walk around looking like they don't "get it."

Recently I happened to spend part of one day with a friend in a chemo lounge of an oncology office, and part of one day at a world-renowned Switzerland-based spa. The people who laughed, poked fun, kidded each other, brought little presents, and had a pleasant bearing were in the chemo lounge; they were also hairless with home-knitted caps and clothes hanging on their too-thin bodies. The people who were grim faced, swaddled in lush robes, with neck warmers and soft booties, impatiently waiting for their back-to-back massage, facials, and aromatherapy, were in the spa.

Attitude management is not to make friends or be nicey-nice in hopes that everyone will be keen on you. They won't. Just as you don't like everyone, not everyone will like you.

Manage your attitude so that people will allow you to lead. Your chosen perspective will cause others to follow you or avoid you.

Leading with a Positive Perspective

Few things in life are one way or another, good or bad, black or white. Your attitude toward life is the way you see or perceive it, and it is based on what you've been taught, plus your socialization, education, and experiences. It's like the little girl who rushed inside her home after her grandpa had taken her to her first professional baseball game and excitedly announced to her parents, "Grandpa gets the best seats. We were higher than everybody."

Take falling in love: you meet someone and talk yourself into how wonderful, smart, kind, handsome or beautiful, or genuine, the person is. Then seven years later on the way to divorce court, you have in your mind only how mean, devious, deceitful, dishonest, and ugly the person is. The person likely didn't change that much, but your perspective did.

Or you join a new company, and you're elated. Great location, title, work, and opportunity, and then two years later you hate the commute, resent the title, distrust your boss, despise the work, and see no opportunity. You can't wait to get out of the place, taking as many paper clips as you can fit in your pockets on your way out the door.

You will be happy in your work life (or in general) to the degree that you can rationalize the perspective you take on it. Some call it "choice blindness," and others call it "manipulated opinion." Regardless, it's up to you.

One CEO friend said, "Your ability to be happy in life is directly related to your ability to rationalize." And another added, "In life you are given a lot of rope. You can climb up it or get it wrapped around your neck, choke, and die. It's your pick."

You can look at everything from one of two viewpoints: what might go right or what might go wrong. Put another way: (1) you can see the opportunity in every difficulty, or (2) you can see the difficulty in every opportunity. Truthfully, you can achieve success with either view, but people will more likely want to have you around if you pick the first option.

One CEO told me this: "I've lost hope in my life twice. I was suicidal because I thought I was alone and didn't have any support system. But once I was out of my immediate doldrums, I realized that feelings are so deceiving. You constantly have to choose the lens you see things through. Your perspective makes it so."

Perspective is everything.

When my mother was alive, she was my best friend. I truly enjoyed her company, and I was appreciative of how I was raised by my dad and her. So I used to do a lot with and for her: buy clothes she wouldn't get for herself, send her on vacations around the world, and give her surprises and treats of any kind that came to mind. One day she said to me, "You do so much for me. It makes me so sad." I was poleaxed. I asked, "What do you mean?" She said, "First, it makes me feel guilty that I didn't do more for my mother when she was alive, and second, it makes me worried and sad for you since you don't have children and no one will do it for you."

Again, perspective is everything.

No matter how clearly you believe you see a situation, everyone else involved can honestly see it from a different perspective. For example, if you get fired tomorrow, is that a bad thing? For you, initially yes, but not for your replacement for whom it's a good thing. And the headhunter who found your replacement gets a fee for the find. The replacement's partner gets a celebratory dinner; the children get a new video game. Your own partner might be relieved because now you both get to move back home and closer to parents. The real estate agent who sells your house gets a new listing. And you end up going to a different company and getting a 25 percent raise instead of the one in your past company that was scheduled for 3 percent.

You achieve an optimistic and easy-to-get-along-with attitude by knowing and accepting yourself; working in a job you have passion in or working in whatever job you have with passion; and valuing and choosing happiness and a bright perspective over dissatisfaction and negative thoughts and feelings. It helps if you have positive responses to the statements listed in the Personal Relevance Reality Check in the Introduction and reproduced below with a different perspective:

- You feel your smarts are getting you somewhere; you're able to use your skills.
- You are sought out.
- You are taken seriously.
- You sense respect for your authority from those above, below, or around you.
- You gain new responsibilities.
- Your ideas to improve work are welcomed.
- You get recognition and praise.
- You get the materials and information you need to do your job.
- Your company encourages your development and gives you opportunities to grow.

Managing Your Mindset

Though they will try, don't let others control your attitude. Most people choose to see the negative, glum, dour, unworkable side of things. But you cannot afford to let them impose their outlook onto you. It's easy to join in on a pity party, as compared to having a positive, proactive attitude of your own.

The old cliché "misery loves company" rings true because downer people want to *bring you down*. If you dismiss this discussion as Pollyannaish, promoting jolly and jest, it isn't. The benefits of managing your own mindset are not just for you. Your mindset affects others, and it improves your chances of reaching a leadership role.

Another reason to fight glum whiners is that negativity is expensive. It costs the country $500 million a year (according to that 2013

Gallup poll I referenced earlier); plus it increases work accidents, absenteeism, and quality defects, while lowering productivity and work performance.

My best friend is fond of saying, "Do what you want to so at least one person is happy." So I say, "Think the way you want to so at least one person thinks that way."

I warn you: a bright, upbeat perspective is more difficult to maintain than a dour one because sometimes things really stink in business. It takes a stronger will to be sanguine; it's easier to be pessimistic. With most things you have one chance at one point in time to make a difference and to stand out. Start doing so today by:

- Choosing a positive temperament even if it's unwarranted.
- Carving out hope when others see none.
- Looking for the best aspect of any situation for the fun of it.
- Expecting good things every morning you wake up.
- Making up your mind to experience that once-a-year feeling that comes from some holiday or specific event every day.
- Pushing sour thoughts and negativity out of your mind.
- Asking yourself every night before bed if you made someone's life better, easier, or happier with your frame of mind.

Garrett McNamara, who holds the Guinness World Record for surfing the world's tallest wave (100 feet), told me he was thinking positive thoughts on the crest: "I just kept telling myself, 'Make it, make it.'" He didn't keep telling himself, "This could get bad, this could get bad."

Perpetual hopefulness helps you achieve your mission, no matter how big or small. You can still consider, prepare, think ahead, and plan for potential mistakes to happen so that you aren't naïve or caught off guard. But if your default mode is can-do in spirit even when you experience frustration, setbacks, and problems, that's your strength of character.

A can-do mindset will help you get more followers, experience longer lasting successes, and triumph over adversity; it will fuel resiliency over negativity and reduce stress. And according to a presentation made by Dr. Dennis Charney of the Mount Sinai School of Medicine, it will make you physically healthier. In addition to Dr. Charney's findings, in 2013 both ABC and NBC news feeds reported that:

- Optimism staves off strokes in older people, is linked to long life, and helps people cope with stress.
- Happiness boosts optimism in people, which increases persistence, which results in their earning an income as much as 30 percent higher.

And as one CEO put it, "Having a positive mental attitude creates a force field around you."

No one cares if you are having a bad day. If you choose a serene and slightly joyful view now, you'll have sanity when things really get difficult. As Warren Buffett likes to say, "The world does not belong to the pessimist. Believe me."

Go beyond good-natured and venture into good-humored. And of course I don't mean humor as in being a stand-up comedian, wearing a red rubber ball on your nose, putting a thumbtack on your boss's chair, or flashing a scary photo onto a coworker's computer screen. By being good-humored, I mean *be human*. Stay positive, and be open to others. If you are optimistic and easy to relate to and get along with, you will positively connect with others (professionally and personally) sooner and in a better way. You will also be able to change the energy of a bad situation, minimize hubris, diffuse negative emotion, relieve tension, reduce burnout, improve morale, enhance cooperation, and even, lower blood pressure—yours and that of the people around you.

Your optimism and friendliness will cause people to want to work with you. You will become a better boss, team member, leader, and family member. No one can give this optimism to you, but no one can take it away either.

CHAPTER 4

Clamor for Information and Insight

To DIFFERENTIATE yourself, you don't have to have an especially high IQ. No matter who you are or what your background or current circumstance is, one thing is certain: you can always learn, explore, and experiment in new arenas. You only need to be reasonably intelligent and insatiably curious. You can *never* know too much; and you can *never* have too much information and insight.

If you do not train yourself constantly to learn about humanity, business, places, and ideas, you are just asking for defeat. As some CEOs weighed in:

- "I can find a lot of ambitious, hardworking people, but I want creativity, and that comes from curiosity. . . . It's a huge turn-off to me if someone isn't curious. It's disorienting."
- "Even if you're number one, you'd better learn something new, and you'd better keep challenging yourself, or they are going to forget about you."
- "I will fire a person who has no ambition to learn on his or her own."

You entered this life with an active brain ready to learn. Discovery is one of a child's first and simplest behaviors, but for adults, it slips into being one of the most underrated behaviors.

Don't let that happen to you. Why? First, following your curiosity will prevent you from being uninformed on a lot of subjects. Second, it will allow you to discover that the "intellectuals" don't have all the answers; people who write for newspapers and magazines and talk on television don't know more than you. And third, it will make you more imaginative, leading to greater creativity. If you're inspired, you'll develop a unique way of looking at day-to-day tasks, problems, opportunities, and even people issues. When you act on what you see—that is, when you act on your vision—innovation will follow.

One beauty of the business world is that everyone is forever a beginner. Experience counts for a great deal, and yet, it counts for very little at the same time. Really, every day we start from scratch, still not quite sure about what we're doing. Being unlimited and insatiable in your inquisitiveness about everything and everyone benefits you and subsequently others. Most everything about business, well, life too, is fluid. Daily you have to deal with the new normal. What got you to this point in your life and career won't necessarily take you further, unless you constantly have your antennae out to learn, sense, and grasp new information. Change has always faced human beings, but with the technology available to us today, it is now happening at warp speed. A voracious love for learning and an appetite for knowledge is a major differentiator.

I asked CEOs for their definition of an "individual who is intellectually curious." They said that the person is someone who:

- Is keenly observant.
- Has an appetite for knowledge.
- Seeks the big picture, and gets a sense of the whole.
- Gets to the bottom of things.
- Has learning agility.
- Expands his knowledge beyond what is required.
- Broadens her mind.
- Has a vigorous intellect.
- Is open-minded.
- Has the right intellectual wattage.
- Is committed to lifelong learning.
- Learns something every single day.
- Has a passion for seeking out different ways of doing things.

One of my favorite quotes in this whole book comes from Curt Carter, CEO of America, Inc.: "I love information. I'm an information freak. The day before I leave this life, I'm going to learn something new. I may not do much with it, but I will have learned it."

There's a television advertisement currently running for a private university with the tagline "Don't miss your one chance to get a good education." That's so wrong. Your chance to get a great education continues until your last breath. Daily you can add to your self-worth: bridge the gap between who, what, and where you are now and who, what, and where you want to be. If you continue every day with the approach that you are a work in progress, you'll find that your growth and development become quite interesting to you and probably to others.

Please note that I'm not talking about your formal education— going back to school and getting another degree or certification. Rather, what I'm talking about is an attitude of interest toward the world. As one CEO told me, "I want smart and creative, but that doesn't mean I'm looking at their GPA."

The person who will go further fastest appoints himself the director of training for himself. After your formal schooling where you were taught what was required for a grade or a degree is largely completed, the world of information is wide open to you—nothing is off limits to your curiosity. You can be a kid again, but now when you go to the candy, record, comic book, or video game store, you discover that you own the entire store. It's all there for you; it will envelop you.

Keep at it all day, every day, if for no other reason than that it is good for you. Research conducted at the Johns Hopkins School of Medicine showed that "lifelong learning can improve your health and decrease your chance of dementia."

Plus, as you educate yourself, you will:

- Improve and train your brain.
- Stay relevant.
- Think more.
- Avoid being intellectually lazy.
- Be better armed for the future.

- Duck the horror of boredom.
- Put a stop to ignorance.
- Dodge being made a fool.
- Connect the dots better.
- Enhance your problem-solving ability.
- Explore new ideas. Get the best ideas.
- See more choices.
- Have something interesting to say.
- Contribute more to your family life.
- Advance your career.
- Get more information with which to make better decisions.
- Challenge the status quo.
- Test old assumptions and change direction where you've been misguided.
- Have a more qualified opinion—a different and broader perspective.
- Add value to your company.
- Better understand others.
- Give yourself a more worldly view.
- Be better prepared for unexpected career interruptions.
- Be better equipped to deliver results when you can link the organization's needs with what you're learning.
- Gain new strategies and methods.
- Have something fresh to talk about at the office or at home with family and friends.
- Increase your chance of knowing what to do next.
- Add to your confidence.
- Avoid mental flabbiness.
- Innovate and create more because you have more knowledge and information to work from.
- Grow, adapt, and evolve.
- Pass on what you learn to others.
- Know what to do when you don't know what to do.

If that list of reasons isn't long enough for you to turn up the juice in this area, I don't know what will get you moving!

The point of continuously increasing your intellectual curiosity is *not* to be superior, show how smart you are, convey an insufficiency in others, put your intelligence on display like a new pair of shoes, use as a weapon, or be clever or vain. It's to grasp everything from anyone and forget nothing.

Use all the brains you have and all you can borrow from all ages of mentors, peers, coaches, bosses, colleagues, competitors, customers, books, seminars—the more diverse the better. One CEO of a men's underwear company stocks his corporate plane with women's magazines. When I asked why he chose those instead of, say, *Men's Fitness*, he explained that it's women who buy his product, and he wanted to understand what they think and know.

So, What to Learn?

First, what's necessary, then what's useful, and then what's fun.

Educators report that around eight years old, you start to determine your own interests. Schooling continuously forces you to be exposed to other areas, but your first tendency is to gravitate to things that pertain to your own personal, developing self.

But don't stop there. Instead, seek out experiences, thoughts, and ideas that aren't considered necessary or useful or that pertain to yourself. Just as the business world is fluid, so too is your own world. It will change, and you will need to be prepared to handle it faster and to stretch into areas you're not sure if you'll need. Nothing is too oddball, irrelevant, immaterial, or unrelated for you. You never know what will be important or how and when you might use it some time.

Don't let your first reaction to an article or seminar on some distant issue be "I'm not curious about _____ because it's not my job." Instead, think, "I could learn about _____ because in the future I may be dealing with it."

So keep your curiosity antennae out for what:

- Pertains to you.
- Doesn't pertain to you.

- Is necessary for this stage of your life.
- Is useful for the next stage of your life.
- Is relevant to what others are uninformed about.
- Is fun now and in the future.
- Is something you can pass on to benefit others.

And specifically regarding your job, be alert for:

- What your boss's goals are.
- How management thinks.
- How the company operates—that is, what the big picture is.
- What your company's capabilities are.
- What your competition is doing.
- What your consumers and customers are thinking and doing.
- What creates value.
- What management expects of you.

Try to gain clarity in truly understanding things instead of being satisfied with what you already know. For every issue, topic, or subject that you encounter, ask yourself, "What am I missing knowing about this? What are others seeing that I don't? What is driving what and why? What is motivating people? Why do these things happen? What's a unique option or solution?" Such questions will encourage creative and innovative thinking.

Your curiosity and agility to learn play a large part in your ability to get hired and promoted. Every CEO or C-suite executive says, "I hire people smarter than I am." One CEO, a former McKinsey & Company consultant and university president, even told me, "I hire people twice as smart as I am."

Ongoing learning will help you in whatever position you're currently in, but just as important, it will prepare you for the job you don't have yet. Someday you might land that bigger job, and when you do, you won't have the time to prepare for the problems that will inevitably come along like strikes of lightning. If you have regularly been learning new skills, considering new ideas, and looking at situations from different angles, you'll find that you have been training your brain to react intuitively to whatever situation or problem arises. This ability will set you apart from other colleagues, managers, and friends who maintain a stagnant state in which they are not constantly learning new things. One CEO told me this: "Sometimes you have six seconds to think about what to do. You can't be searching your conscious competence. You had better have unconscious competence." He expanded on this point with the following story:

I was a very junior guy who had just joined the company, but I decided to learn about my CEO who was some 14 levels above me. I remember figuring out that he made 354 times my salary. . . . Since I worked for a public company, I could read the CEO's letter in the annual report. I read the previous five years letters. I wanted to learn if what he said he was going to do, he did. Did he present an understandable explanation of the business? Did he show progress toward goals? Did he have smart strategies for the future? I realized that a CEO's letter is often written by the communications department and can be full of confusing jargon and irrelevant fluff, but I figured if I read my company's CEO's letters over a span of several years, I'd garner some valuable information and insight.

In addition, I paid attention to every action or inaction that he took and that I was privy to through internal communication, articles written about him, and interviews that he did. I intensely watched to see what clothes he wore, how he presented himself, whom he let interview him, whom he talked to, how he treated mistakes, whom he hired and promoted, what he put up with, and what he rewarded. I tried to learn all I could about the human being behind the public job because I knew it would profoundly affect the corporate culture and my future.

When the opportunity came up to present to him, I didn't go in as this junior guy with my hat in hand. Instead, I said, "Here's what I'm doing and proposing. . . . I hope you have time and interest to be part of it. . . ." I knew more about how he'd answer than he knew, and he became an avid sponsor of my career.

At a young age I knew that I wanted to be in charge. I wanted to run the show. I took all kinds of courses on my own. Read books on all aspects of leadership and being a CEO. I'd get one good idea per book and then find other people and get their approach on that idea. I was always thinking about how I could embody this and actively practice it. With every job I got a little more of the show, and I ran the best show I could with the part of the show that I had. Eventually I got the whole show.

A different company head told me that when he started with a new group, he researched the entire executive team and learned the routes each took to get into their positions: "I studied up and down and all around, mapped out the personnel selection method, and deconstructed the whole process so that I knew the path that I needed to take to the CEO position."

Take a look at your own company's written core competencies, and make sure you meet them. Some common competencies include the following:

- Has a creative and innovative management style
- Has strategic agility
- Manages with vision and purpose
- Keeps the focus on the customers
- Can build effective teams
- Can motivate others
- Is driven to get results
- Is able to deal with ambiguity
- Acts with integrity and trustworthiness
- Can delegate

Those are the "must-haves" that nearly all companies value. Next, you have to dig deeper to understand exactly what those competencies mean in your environment. Take "manages with vision and purpose" and learn what that really means. One company I've worked with defined it this way:

The person communicates a compelling and inspired vision and has a sense of the core purpose for the organization. The person talks about his or her team's ideas beyond those of just today and looks at the possibilities for the future. The person is optimistic about the vision and purpose and creates mileposts and symbols such that his or her constituents can rally support behind it, and it's shared by everyone. His or her communication and manner motivate beyond his or her direct reports and engage the whole organization.

Still vague and a little generic, right? Ask questions like these:

- What was the vision five years ago?
- Who spearheaded it?
- What made it happen? What caused it to fail?
- What were the mileposts and symbols that garnered support?
- What was the next core sense of purpose?
- What are other department heads' vision?
- What are other companies in your industry doing?
- What are other progressive companies in other industries doing?
- Who spearheads the successful outcomes?
- What caused those successful outcomes in other companies and in other industries?

Continuous learning should trigger thinking. That's the whole point of it!

Unfortunately our broad use of technology too often debilitates our thinking. I saw a product advertisement with the tag line: "You don't have to think. We've done it for you." And I thought that it was so not right. We need to fight against that. A quick online search showed me that 89 percent of people use search engines to answer questions. I'm all for using search engine tools, but to differentiate yourself, talk to others, observe, and ruminate. Debate with people you think are smart so that you can get the information and reasoning that others who are relying solely on technology can't get.

Learn things that matter, and deduce things no one else does. Don't just acquire information. Think about how you make sense of it and use it too.

Career criminals do this all the time. I interviewed a habitual offender who told me that every day he learned something new from his fellow inmates: how to hotwire a car, get around a house alarm, self-tattoo, fake an ID, skirt possession laws, get out of handcuffs, avoid detection in a break-in, smuggle contraband into the prison, use sign language for times he wasn't allowed to speak, and some more disgusting things I won't relay. Of course, it's not just career criminals who spend time learning.

Right now your biggest competitor is likely studying your weaknesses, vulnerabilities, and limitations. Colleagues, team members, subordinates, and even bosses are closely watching and observing you, trying to find areas in which you are lacking, so that they can prevail over you when the next promotion comes around. Oh, and by the way, you better be doing the same thing to them. To get the nod, you have to do more, have more, and be more than the next person. This is not to climb or crawl all over other people. This is to climb, crawl, and leap over yourself. This competitiveness happens in boardrooms, backrooms, and bars. Done well, the way I'm writing about in this book, causes all ships to rise, meaning that you will succeed as you help others—a trait to differentiate yourself that is discussed in Chapter 12.

Turn Up the Juice in Your Reading, Talking, and Writing

Experts will tell you that worldwide, there are three dominant learning styles: listening, seeing, and experiencing. From self-reflection, such as occurred when you wrote your life story, you can discover your most used and powerful method. After learning what is necessary and useful in your immediate job, you can then go beyond your dominant method of learning. For example, let's say you had to give a presentation on your project at a company off-site. Your usual style, the "experiencing style," is to dive right in, write it, practice it, and deliver it. But instead, you could go beyond your usual style. You could call a friend (or someone not so friendly but who has made good presentations) and ask her about her preparation process. Listen to what she has to say, without your own pontificating, and then watch her make a live presentation or watch her on a Vimeo recording. You can learn presentation techniques from other sources, too, such as TED talks and professional seminars. Take notice of what interests, attracts, or impresses you, and watch what the audience reacts positively to.

Don't stop growing your intellectual curiosity, and don't satisfy it in only one way, either. The following actions will help you to continue learning and stay on your toes in your professional and private life.

Read Voraciously

Always be reading, even if it's speed reading the Internet, magazines, papers, news websites, industry publications, or books. One young woman in the fashion industry told me she listens to podcasts at triple speed. (You can always slow down and review what you've read or listened to if you need or want to improve your understanding of the material.)

Be a critical reader. Don't filter out thoughts, ideas, or information that at first glance seems irrelevant to you or that you disagree with. Read comparatively—two books by different CEOs at the same time, for example. You'll see how people in similar roles at similar levels of responsibility approach their work differently, which will provide a new perspective on how you perform your work as well. If you read in a second language, read the same book in each language to compare and contrast the original with the translation. Discover how one translator interpreted the material in comparison to how you did.

Such exercises get you to do things differently, see things differently, and then act differently from others. These exercises will help you get out of thought ruts and lazybones actions that make your life boring and dull, and they will also help you become more productive.

Read with a purpose. Don't read words for information alone but rather, to help you make sense out of patterns. Read for contrary opinions, and read just to ruminate.

Sometimes you'll benefit from systematically, thoughtfully, and closely reflecting on what you're reading paragraph by paragraph. Pick something valuable out of everything, and experiment with how you can apply it. Go further than you have to—to have fun, to test, and to end up with an unexpected outcome.

Whether you do it to stay contemporary, enrich your memory, or develop new ideas, reading is the least expensive and most flexible education tool out there. From reading 15 minutes a day, you will see results in a year. Even 4 minutes a day of disciplined intent and focus on listening, seeing, or experiencing beyond what's necessary will have created by the end of the year over 24 hours of self-improvement and development.

One CEO told me this: "I spend a great deal of time getting information, reading everything from scientific journals to daily news, watching YouTube videos, and traveling to meet and talk with colleagues. I'm continuously educating myself. . . . I don't do it for a job promotion. I'm the CEO already. I do it to encapsulate everything I've learned so I can communicate." Another CEO gave his perspective: "I try to read everything of some one thing and something of everything."

Shockingly and sadly, according to BookStatistics.com, "42 percent of college graduates never read another book after college." And according to a poll from the Associated Press-Ipsos, "One in four adults has read no books at all in the last year." If you make the small effort of simply reading occasionally, you're setting yourself apart from others.

Rub Your Brain Up Against Others: Talk to People!

One entrepreneur told me this story:

> I owned a retail store next to a Walmart some years ago, and there was an issue I wanted to discuss with them. Normally a lawyer, papers, and letters would be involved. But I didn't want the typical approach, so I called Walmart headquarters and asked to speak to the person who handled real estate, fully expecting to get a midlevel facilities manager. The secretary said, "Okay," and the next thing I knew some guy answered, "Sam here." I asked, "Sam Walton?"

He said, "Yes," so I told him about the issue, and Sam said he'd look into it. He did, and he had someone get back to me. If I hadn't made the call, I wouldn't have ever gotten to talk to the legend.

Talk to people you don't know, do know, shouldn't talk to, or normally wouldn't. And actually talk. Don't just text! Talking to people will not only make others feel valued but it will also help you learn about the different ways that people were brought up and think. You build up your own comfort level and self-confidence when you engage with others you normally wouldn't. It is painless and interesting. And you just might acquire some new or helpful information. You should avoid being a standoffish, aloof, and disinterested person. (Believe me, you do not come across as James Dean or James Franco cool.)

Don't just speak to those you know and like or those you think like you. Talk to people who think differently from you. One CEO I know mans the customer complaint line for a couple of hours at least one day a month. Another told me he spends 10 minutes a day with the guy who fixes his car and with the guy who rakes his leaves "just to keep it real because they are our company's customers."

Talk to people to enlarge, connect, or improve on what you know. Open your mind in the conversation. Don't try to shine with your wit. Help those you're speaking with shine with theirs.

Ask: "What's in the pipeline?" "What are you envisioning in the [next year]?" "What do you think about [a particular issue]?" "Can you tell me more about that?" Discern trends. Get a sense of the future. Look for the "white space" where there is opportunity.

If you pay attention, you'll always learn something.

The late Peter Georgescu, the former chairperson emeritus of Young & Rubicam, told me: "I like to sit on a plane and talk to strangers. I don't want to talk to Jack Welch, Moses, or Jesus Christ. You can learn an enormous amount from the average person."

It's just like a young, amiable-looking, business-attired, clean-shaven man I saw once on a street corner in Athens, Greece, years ago. (Note, not a street person looking for handouts.) I noticed he spoke a few friendly greeting words to every single woman walking by him (young or old) as if he knew her. I wondered if he in fact knew every woman who passed so I went up to him and asked if in fact he was acquainted with them all and if that was why he could so easily talk to them. He responded this way: "The reason I talk to everyone is because I may never get the chance again." We talked a little longer, and I found out he was in finance. On his lunch break, he always brought a sandwich to this park and then spent a few minutes going out of his way to initiate a conversation with someone. Now it's worth noting that he put more effort into talking to the women than to the men, but still he talked to people he didn't know and maybe shouldn't have in some people's eyes.

One CEO I know takes a sabbatical every seven years to spend six months in Bali. Nice idea, but practically speaking most of us don't have the resources to do that. But in our diverse workforce, you can talk to somebody from Bali in person, or at least online, without the price of airfare. My point is that, in these modern times, you in your cubicle or corner office have the same potential to listen to and learn from, and about, people halfway around the world.

During business travel in California, I found myself at the same hotel as the New England Patriots football team. I quickly read up about them online so that I could recognize the players—although it was sort of easy based on each player's size alone. Then I rode up and down the elevator as frequently as possible (trying not to look too weird), spent time in the lobby and restaurants where the players tended to gather, and, when possible, engaged in conversation with them. I explained that I was an executive coach and I was interested in their world of sports coaching. They willingly volunteered what they liked, didn't like, had learned, and planned to teach others if they ever got into coaching football.

No matter who you're with or where you are or what you're doing, you can always learn something. Make it your private mission to garner one new piece of information, insight, or intrigue from a person every hour of your day. View it as your private workshop or laboratory. Can you imagine what you could do with that much information? It's exciting to think about!

Write Down What You Learn

Writing down what you learn is a sound way to help remember new concepts, sort out ideas, and share what you've found. I know you think you will remember everything you read or discuss, but you simply can't. Writing forces you to be more exact than you would be in just keeping the thoughts in your head. "To write well is to think well" is a cliché your English teacher probably taught you. But cliché or not, there is a lot of truth to it. Putting thoughts down on paper, and even posting or tweeting your thoughts, causes you to concentrate. Scientists say that your memory of something improves as you write it down because in doing so, you get to view it more than once.

When you put pen to paper, especially handwriting instead of typing, you reinforce the information in your subconscious. Acupuncturists say holding the pen or pencil invigorates massage points that stimulate thinking.

Write your life story, write your accomplishments, write your goals, write your thoughts and observations, write what you want to teach your children, and write just to write. Most people won't do this. You should. Your writings can always be used for something worthwhile.

Never Stop Learning

A vigorous intellect always gathering information is a gift you give to yourself. You can learn a little every day, and over the course of a year you've completely altered your life.

You have a right to wake up smarter each morning. Every time you add something to your brain, you add to your self-worth.

Don't just read through this part and say, "Oh, yeah, good reminder." Instead, consciously do something about it by making a mental note at the end of the day: "What do I know now that I didn't when the day started?"

If you can't specifically point to something you learned today, you probably didn't learn anything.

But if you can point to an idea, procedure, strategy, or activity that helps you add value to your company, better understand others or a situation, connect the dots on a project, have a more qualified opinion, make a better decision, solve a pressing problem, give yourself and your group a wider worldly view, be more prepared for the unexpected, readjust old assumptions to new thinking—if you can do any of these and can pass some or all of it on to others, you will differentiate yourself. You will stand out and be sought out from above when promotions are being considered and from below when people are looking for leaders.

PART II

How to Differentiate Your Being

CHAPTER 5

Look Your Best

THERE IS one main reason to be conscious of your physicality and appearance: because everyone else is.

People are always watching, and the higher your position in an organization, the more eyes are on you—sometimes to size you up, sometimes to learn and emulate, and sometimes to look out for your slipups.

One manager told me he makes a note after a candidate's job interview as to whether the person cleans up the coffee cup that was used during the conversation or leaves it for someone else to pick up. Years ago a manager told me about an employee's missing out on a job advancement because the boss had spotted him in the company cafeteria with dirty inside pockets on his khakis, which was visible when he sat down, and the manager didn't want that representing him. The same boss didn't like a female colleague wearing a combination of gold and silver jewelry instead of one or the other.

I realize that these seem trivial, but apparently they weren't to that particular boss—maybe that is what his mom and dad taught him. When I told this story to one CEO, he responded, "It's a really rotten leader if his main concern is whether someone wears a new suit of clothes and has his shoes shined."

It may not be morally right or politically correct to judge by appearances, but it still happens moment by moment, hour by hour.

In defense of the nitpicking CEO: just as a company's logo, packaging, and product all help to communicate how a company wants the customer to perceive it, your appearances and actions are the logo and packaging of your product; they similarly communicate how you will be identified. My guess is that you want to be viewed as memorable, impressive, credible, genuine, trusted, comfortable, competent, and confident; straightforward, not manipulative; reliable and dependable; and different and better than your competition.

Sometimes What Is Not Discussed Needs to Be Discussed

Much of this chapter is about everything your boss cannot legally talk about with you. He wants to, but he can't and won't for fear of being sued if he compliments you or charged with harassment if he criticizes. Yet your appearance forms a first and lasting impression. It is a standard that people judge you by, and it is the reality of part of what gets you hired or promoted.

It's how you conduct yourself in your physicality: manner, head, eyes, face, voice posture, pacing, and dress. People believe that what is going on inside your head is revealed by your persona. They say things like this all the time: "I'm a good judge of character." "I can read people well." "I just see someone, and I know whether I can trust him." They conclude based on what you show them, either on purpose or accidentally, with your forethought or without in how you physically comport yourself. This chapter will ensure that what you show them is done with awareness and responsibility.

Some physical distinctions are accidental—height, color, beauty, and facial symmetry, for example. What you do with them is the differentiator. One grand dame in the cosmetics world was famous for saying, "There are no ugly women. Only lazy ones."

People believe what they see—based on their frame of reference— and even if you feel and talk a good game of confidence and competence, if you don't show it in your comportment, no one will accept it as true. Studies show that over 80 percent of what people believe and remember they received visually.

We all know that there is an expected "look" of a rock 'n' roll star: wildly shaking his hairy head, looking surly, followed with jumping up and down across the stage with a guitar waddling in front of him soon to be busted into pieces at the climax of the show. Similarly there's an expected look of a leader, too.

Your physical appearance and comportment are what people use to judge you, size you up, and pigeonhole you. You do it to others; others do it to you. It's not fair, but neither is life.

Most of us were raised on television and know that even with the mute button on, we can watch the characters and pretty much follow the story line. We can tell what the actors are likely going to do next by how they stand, sit, walk, shrug, smirk, smile, gesture, hunch, and so on. That's where we start to learn to "act" ourselves. From massive media exposure, we learn that there is a "look" to a confident and competent individual. He's someone who appears comfortable in his own skin, stands upright, maintains direct eye contact, is unharried, and speaks in a way that is easy to hear.

Dr. Paul Ekman, professor of psychology at the University of California, is considered the world's foremost face reader. As part of his research, he showed pictures with varying facial expressions to people in the United States, Japan, Argentina, Chile, Brazil, and even the highlands of Papua, New Guinea, where there was no television to bias the respondents' answers. He found that all people judged the expressions in the same way as to whether the person photographed was, for example, angry or happy. He found that universally, even without massive media exposure and starting at a very young age, we are very savvy in seeing distinctions in deportment.

It seems incongruous in this digital age to write about the value of a person's physicality since so much interaction is online, but it's precisely that reason why it's extra important now. You have infrequent face-to-face contact with colleagues, your network of connections, even your bosses, so when it does happen, you need to make sure that you send the message you intend.

Here are some descriptions I've heard from bosses expressing what bothers them about some employees when seen in person:

- "Walks into the room like a loser, not the senior manager she is."
- "Runs his hands through his hair, adjusts his shirt collar, darts his eyes around the room, shoots his mouth off meaninglessly, and fidgets in every way."

- "Doesn't have an executive laugh. She snorts."
- "Is lazy about his appearance. Doesn't appear to have brushed his hair, and wears rumpled clothes."
- "Seems insecure in how he walks and talks; he's defensive and protective."
- "Needs to smile more."
- "He's always glancing at his watch when in a meeting."
- "He looked good on paper, but he came in not showing his best: wrinkled clothes, visible tattoos, and a nose ring."
- "His appearance definitely affected my promotion decision despite his qualifications."
- "Talks, dresses, and acts like a cast member from *Jersey Shore*."

These comments were said during private conversations but not to the person. The boss isn't allowed to say a lot of these things to you. Human resources instruct them not to. So if you wonder if any of this is holding you back, you have to initiate the conversation. Even then, expect the filtered truth. As one CEO told me, "There are lots of acts of kindness to help someone out that aren't permitted anymore."

Your actions don't have to be as egregious as the ones in the list. If you smirk, roll your eyes, sigh often and deeply, or stare at your phone on your lap under the desk, you will be noticed, but not in a good way. What seems inconsequential isn't to others. Even a micronod or a nanosmile is read, interpreted, judged, and reacted to.

Only if you get someone's positive attention can you then make your compelling position be heard. Changing just a few habits can add a measurable impact to your presence—and we aren't talking bright white teeth and a tan. We're talking about self-awareness and discipline: you don't even have to say a word; your manner communicates your energy, attitude, confidence, and competence.

Be Comfortable in Your Skin, Even If You're Acting a Part

Do not protest with, "Discussing the importance of physicality over productivity is fake! I want to be genuine and transparent and real." All I can politely say is, "You're misguided."

Every day, all day long, each one of us "acts" for whatever role we are playing at the time: spouse, friend, parent, boss, subordinate, buyer, supplier, interviewer, interviewee, mentor, coach, and so forth. I prefer to call it learning, maturing, adapting, and taking responsibility for your effect on others, not acting.

Some CEO comments:

- "I was told that I look as though I've been a CEO all my life, . . . but what I really feel is that I sometimes have to hide my crazy. My wife calls it my mental Botox. It's my mask of serenity to hide my emotions."
- "My kids think I built my career on sage nodding."
- "I've been told I have important-looking eyebrows."
- "You're scared all the time, and yet you have to hide it. It's the price you pay to play the game."

As discussed in the first part of the book, if you pretend to be who and what you want to be and behave accordingly, one day you will finally become that person. To appear as this person to others is the initial goal.

A business leader I know who is frequently on television was giving a speech that was being covered by the media. He'd speak and pose in an odd position for seemingly no reason: raise his eyebrows while making an interesting point; move to stand with legs apart in defiance; massage his forehead, the bridge of his nose, or earlobes at various points to show his unease; open his hands to demonstrate openness to new ideas; and key up his voice to deliver an expression. When watching all of this as part of the audience, his actions seemed unrelated. Later, I saw the local newscast, and those exact poses and sound bites were what were featured. He knew exactly how to act to be camera friendly and interesting to the media. He was the stereotype of what we expect a leader to look and act like.

I remember attending a congressional meeting where the CEO I had accompanied was testifying before a subcommittee seeking funding for his medical charity. I met him on the steps of Congress ready to go into the meeting, and he was sporting a safety pin holding his eyeglasses together. You couldn't help noticing, so I asked if he had a way to get them fixed. He responded, "No, I want them this way." It was part of the effect he wanted to have on the people he was presenting to. He did it for a number of reasons: to stand out from what they expected in someone coming to them and trying to impress them to get what they wanted. He was trying to differentiate himself from the others who are always camera ready. Instead, he wanted to fit in with the sense of "needing funding and support"—as his glasses needed repair.

As mentioned, your boss won't have this discussion with you because human resources won't allow it, even though he'd like to. Keep this in mind. The second reason I am highlighting this point is that as you get older, you have a tendency to make this concept less important, though it's actually the most imperative time to physically differentiate yourself.

Keep Your Head About You

We like level-headed executives—literally and figuratively.

When you are strong, certain, and confident, your head is likely to be straight up. But when you are tired, uncertain, needy, or scared, you are likely to tilt your head to one side, making you look meek and timid like a whipped dog or a begging child. Just as people judge honesty by whether you "look them in the eye," they judge confidence, even competence by looking at how tilted your head is.

Keep a Level Head

Tilting one way or another over time is going to cause you chiropractic problems, even chronic neck, back, and head aches. But more important, it sends out signals of weakness, fear, and insecurity—whether those are there or not. So right now, check whether one of your ears is closer to the corresponding shoulder or not and adjust accordingly. Some people have lived with an angled head for so long their eyes adjust to reading askew, and when they straighten their neck and try to read, it takes a while to adjust.

Just as you can't judge a CD (or a book) by its cover, you can't or shouldn't judge others by something as insignificant as their head holding habit. But bear in mind that they are likely judging you by that simple physicality. So be aware of and take responsibility for micromovements from your head on down.

The bottom line: in corporate America "heads up" can mean a lot of things—your thinking, your preparation, or your physical posture. People describe character based on what they see physically: head on straight, looks you in the eye, stands on her own two feet, can't look you in the eye, spineless, gutless, two-faced, plus numerous other pejorative expressions. If you're going to work to be good at so many important things, don't let something minor like this get in your way.

Most times in professional development consulting, my work isn't to change people but to get them to stop sabotaging themselves, getting in their own way, shooting themselves in the foot—and that's what a small thing like the tilted head does.

Chin up, chin down, head tilted to the left or to the right, face turned to the left or the right when talking, forcing you to look at a person out of the corner of your eyes instead of looking straight on, or a combination of any of those hurts your impact.

Now if you are consoling a coworker who just lost his mother to cancer, its fine to have your head at a sympathetic angle. But you don't want to have that same position when you are confronting your competition or presenting to the executive committee.

Stop the Bobblehead

Along with the nonlevel head, excessive bobbing and nodding should be curtailed. Watch a group of people at an office cocktail party. People's heads are bouncing like they are part of a bobblehead doll convention and looking like a spring-neck-dog in the back window of a 1957 Chevy. It looks too agreeable, easy, accepting, nervous, subservient, and lacking in confidence. Do the opposite of what most people do: substitute one slow, deep nod or a micronod. Better yet, don't nod at all, but instead offer a "verbal nod" like: "Well done." "I see your point." "Good job."

Excessive bobbing up and down can be a rare neurological movement disorder, one that requires a surgical repair. Luckily for most of us, all that's required is awareness and the discipline to stop it.

In the whole scheme of workplace etiquette and your life, none of this should matter, but it does, and the impact of doing some minute thing one way or another often lasts a long time.

Wear an Open, Easygoing Facial Expression

You can be taken seriously even if you indiscriminately smile out loud.

This concept is all about your "game face." Keep an awake, alert, alive look that invites people to talk to you. Why? Because you need people to talk to you with suggestions, problems, advice, watch-outs, issues, mistakes, concerns, opportunities, fears, and frustrations. If they don't talk to you because you present yourself as closed, shut off, uninterested, bored, confrontational, and downright scary, you are the one who loses. And when I say lose, I mean that people won't interpret you correctly. They might mistakenly assume your intent, and you may not get credit for your true thoughts. As mistaken as their impression of you may be, it might cause them to react differently from what you expected or wanted in the communication exchange. And it was your fault for not taking responsibility for making sure that your actions were consistent with the message you intended.

An open face, especially sporting an easy smile, makes you look approachable and approving of others—"You're okay; I'm okay." You give people a lift and convey the impression that things are sinking in, not bouncing off of you. An expressionless flat face or a smirk, sneer, or even slightly pursed lips says, "You *are not* okay; *I'm* okay." Besides, if you keep at it, as you get older, you'll get mean lines around your mouth, and you'll scare your grandchildren away.

A cheerful face displays self-assurance and gives a bearing of easy authority. You give the impression of being fearless, comfortable, competent, cool, calm, and collected under pressure. With confidence and agreeable features on your face, few situations are insurmountable. There's a whole menu of looks you can use: an open smile, easy smile, cooperative smile, expectant smile, knowing smile, caring smile, teasing smile, friendly smile, fearless smile, lingering smile, happy smile, relieved smile, grateful smile, and tense smile.

A calm look on your face helps you avoid wearing your emotions on your sleeve, and it can help you restrain a gut reaction you don't want to show. People can't tell exactly how you are feeling, and that gives you time to think and decide what you are feeling and how much you want to present those feelings.

The problem with most facial expressions is that the outside looks like it is revealing what is going on inside, when in fact it's not. Most people have a relatively happy life, but they seem miserable, walking around looking like they are in pain or severely constipated.

A number of individuals look as though they've never smiled a day in their life or they've been instructed not to smile or they think "the sterner you look, the more you come across as a decisive problem solver," as one manager told me. Some people seem to have a mouth that wants to smile but won't.

For their role-playing purposes, some people try to act more grim and mean than they really are. One CEO told me, "When I walk down the hallway in my company, subordinates scatter like birds at a feeder. . . . It makes me uncomfortable, but if I had a choice, I'd probably avoid me too."

Just stride down the street, airport concourse, or office hallway with a level head and an easy smile, and watch the reaction you get when you substitute an open face for the jutting jaw, frown, dead, flat, dull-eyed like a potato, snarly, flaccid, sour, droopy, shriveled face that looks as if your jaw is wired shut into a catatonic state.

You can keep the mad mug and glum look if you're at a military funeral, in handcuffs headed to prison, or having a mug shot taken. But for everything else, put a genial expression on your face.

A nonsmiling face signals lots of ills. It's worthwhile to know that medical experts say one of the initial signs of dementia is the inability to smile. And when specialists check for signs of a stroke, the first thing they ask the person to do is to try to smile.

Sick, scared, insecure people don't smile; secure people do. Losers don't smile; winners do.

Start by Smiling in Your Mind

Smiling on the inside isn't enough. You also have to notify your face of your intent.

I'm not asking you to sport a big Miss Universe smile, a jubilant beam of winning the Super Bowl, or a face-splitting grin from your fantasy football picks. I'm just looking for an easy, open countenance on your face with your lips slightly parted and the corners of your mouth pulled up a little instead of lazily or habitually pulled downward. You never hear people say the word "grimace" before a photo is taken of them—but you'd think they had. Try saying the word right now—"grimace"—and note the position of the corners of your lips: they are turned down into a frown (like the expression most people walk around with).

The photographer's customary instruction to say "cheese" still works, as do the words "cheese-whiz," "money," "sex," and even "eggplant" to get you to smile. Saying any of these words causes the corners of your lips to lift up a little with the mouth open while engaging the muscles around your eyes. This facial position relaxes your jaw and opens your throat, which improves your voice volume and quality. You'll avoid grinding your teeth as well, which will make your dentist happy.

Keep the Expression Regardless of the Situation

The key to the honest, open, easy smile is to maintain the pleasant-looking and pleasant-feeling expression with your eyes and lips when you are mad, glad, sad, scared, happy, or not; have a headache or a hang nail; are going bald; or going through a divorce. To do it just when things are wonderful would make for a nonsmiling nation. Instead, you do it any time you are outside of a locked bathroom, despite how you feel.

Most electronic transmissions are only a step up from awful. No matter how effective online communication is currently, or will become, it will never surpass face-to-face interaction. Nuance, smell, touch, sight, and sound all add to deeper understanding between people. The human condition has been honed through thousands of years of reading each other. Relatively speaking, we are neophytes in detecting small differences in phone calls, e-mails, texts, or videos. Regardless, whatever you do will come across better with a smile in your head and on your face whether anyone sees it or not. Keep amiable features on your face when you leave a phone message, record your outgoing voice mail message, are participating in an audio or video conference, and even when you type an e-mail—although I am not promoting the use of emoticons such as ☺. So many people use them now that it's more unusual to express the same sentiment in the careful selection of the right words.

Consistency is important. Think about it. Say you're sitting in a meeting with the flat face of most of corporate America and your boss cracks a joke, so you go into a big grin and then back to the flat face. Frankly, you look like a suck-up. Instead, if you have an open-face small smile while listening, when the boss cracks a joke and you laugh and then return to your open-face smile, you will appear authentic and genuine.

Look at restaurant waiters who come to your table with a big smile announcing "today's special," then turn and drop their greeting face and glumly walk away. Their enthusiasm for the "special" or their work doesn't look very sincere, does it? Well, it's the same on your face if you turn your pleasant expression on and off.

Say what you need to say and smile a lot. Give orders with a smile, give critiques, ask questions, say "no," and listen quietly, always with the unconcerned, relaxed, comfortable, competent, confident expression.

You don't want people to have to strain to get a smile from you. They may not bother to do so, and you're the one who loses. Others aren't here to "make your day"—you're here to make theirs, if anything. And as we discussed earlier, if you're difficult to get along with—or appear to be—people won't bother. You have to be very special to cause them to work hard to bring out the good-natured person hovering deep down inside of you. It's better for you to keep the recommended facial expression with your mouth slightly open. The mouth or lips slightly open is not just for when you speak but also for when you listen so that you will *look* like you are listening.

Remove the smirk, pursed lips, slanted sneer, folded lips, tight-lipped, mean thin line, mouth open like a freshwater trout, or facial gyration like something is stuck in the back of a tooth.

Go down any big or small city street any time of the day, and you'll see that 99.99 percent of the people do not have a pleasant look on their face, much less a friendly one. That is reason alone to stand out from the rest. Some people might say that "'pleasant' is in the eye of the beholder." So let me clarify: the best universal illustration of the genial features, pleasant expression, open face, and easy smile that I'm writing about is to imagine you are holding a baby in your arms and take note of your expression. That's what I'm talking about; that's the approving expression that you should be striving for.

From some CEOs I heard these comments:

- "I'm basically shy and not outgoing so I get poker faced, which comes across as formidable and even frightening, which causes people to steer clear. It's not a good thing. I have to fight against what people call my 'emotionless gaze.'"
- "I have high self-confidence but also a healthy level of cynicism. The cynicism keeps me from getting blind-sided, and the bigger my company has grown, the bigger my cynicism has grown too. That's why I look so unpleasant. I'm really being defensive. I need to protect myself and my organization."
- "My assertiveness is really aggressiveness with a smile."
- "I have a manager now who would be a great senior executive if only he'd smile more."
- "I struggle with wearing a smile, or at least not sporting a frown. It isn't as easy as it sounds."
- "Sometimes when I talk, the only thing I'm armed with is a warm smile."

Regardless of your role, you can arrange your face into a certain expression and actually feel the corresponding emotion. In other words, emotions work from the outside in as well as from the inside out. Think about when you are angry or disgusted. It shows all over your face. The problem is, when you are happy, it's not projected in the same way unless you put a little more effort in.

Researchers at the University of Kansas set out to test if the facial expressions we exhibit influence our emotions, and they reported their findings in the journal *Physiological Science*. They placed participants in a stressful situation and instructed them to maintain *neutral, forced,* or *Duchenne* (legitimately joyful, engaging the muscles around the mouth and eyes) *smiles*, some of which were assisted by chopsticks to keep the expression in place. They found the people who smiled, even if forced by chopsticks, had a faster recovery from stress than those with neutral expressions and that the people who smiled because they wanted to reported the greatest recovery, and their heart rates returned to normal the quickest.

More from my own life story . . .

In the spirit of full disclosure, my study of physicality started when I decided to enter pageants as a teen in hopes of earning college scholarships. The big takeaway from the experience was that you learn to walk across a stage, half-naked in a bathing suit, trying to look relaxed and happy to be there. I discovered later in life that every time I walked into a boss's office, interviewed for a job, pitched a sales account, or presented a speech, I was feeling like I was doing the exact same thing.

Another thing that came back to me while writing . . .

As a teen, I spent a lot of time with my parents instead of friends. The reason was simple: my parents were more fun. But it wasn't exactly cool to go places with them at that age. I remember being in line at the movie theater one Saturday night with my dad, and I studied the other kids on dates. The girls were giggly-looking, smiling at the boys, laughing at the (likely) inane humor. So I decided to put extra effort into being happy, smiling, and laughing with my dad instead of wearing a surly look that teenagers can easily take on. Of course, my demeanor made him happy, but the interesting outcome for me was that it made me happier, more comfortable, and more confident.

There is nothing better for your mindset or others than doing good work and smiling the whole time.

People think you smile at a person, but no, you smile at the world. The people nearby might think your smile is directed toward them, and that's okay. But most important, you smile to communicate your confidence. And if people are watching, which they are, you both benefit.

Look 'Em in the Eye or Anywhere Else About the Head

Eyes are powerful in communicating; no other body parts communicate quite the same. The quickest way to look uninterested, distracted, inattentive, or dishonest is to not meet the other person's eyes or even face.

Though most of us are taught to look people in the eye when speaking with them, few do it. People will liberally notice and comment on other people's character with observations such as, "He can't look you in the eye." "She *can* look you in the eye." "He's shifty eyed." "She gives you the evil eye." "He's wild-eyed . . . dull eyed . . . has lies in his eyes." Their impressions cause them to jump to conclusions about other people, even if they are grossly inaccurate.

If you think CEOs with all their important work don't bother with minutiae like eye contact, consider these comments I heard in my interviews:

- "Only if you are Justin Bieber can you afford to divert your eyes, keep moving, never smile, never engage when you meet me in the hallway."
- "I fire eye rollers."
- "Sometimes I purposefully look like I'm asleep in a video conference to see if people might say things they wouldn't say in front of me if I were awake."
- "Eyes speak volumes to me. It's what I trust."
- "Don't look down. You have to face the people you're torturing."
- "If you are always looking around, up, and down, then you better look out in more ways than one."
- "When I'm dealing with difficult people, I look them in the eye and wiggle my eyebrows."

When you are in a conversation, look at the other person's head and face, hairline, ears, eyes, eyebrows, nose bridge, mouth, or of course, eyes. You will look attentive, as if you are interested in them and listening to them, and you will look confident, personable, competent, powerful, and honest.

Meet people's gaze if they are looking at you. Even if they don't maintain eye contact with you, give it to them anyway. Frequently people are as uncomfortable giving eye contact as they are in receiving it. If you attempt a focused attentive expression toward people and they nervously look away, don't divert. By looking away, they are controlling you consciously or unconsciously. If you change direction at that point, you will look and often feel nervous, and you will have less confidence in the interaction. Be steady but not piercing, attentive but not staring. Think about how babies look at you: it's a fixed focus, unwavering, undistracted, just interested and nonjudgmental.

Or think about your dog. Does your dog not give the best eye contact to you, staring with adoration with those big brown eyes? Think about what would happen if you gave eye contact that way to your boss—or at least your significant other!

If you give more, you'll likely get more as well. If you tune in to people with your eyes, you'll likely hear deeper and longer because the tiny bit of extra physical effort seems to deepen the intensity of your hearing. When you've really heard something, you remember it long, and very important, you make the other person feel acknowledged. It's sort of like when you meet someone new and then can't remember the person's name. The cause is less likely to be poor memory than it is that you actually didn't hear the name. When you shake hands and exchange names, the only name you really hear is your own. Next time you meet someone new, closely observe your attention to the other person's words as compared to paying attention to just your own. And whether meeting the first time or the twenty-first time, smile with your eyes as you engage; a stone-faced stare comes across as a hostile glare.

To avoid staring, periodically pause in thought or weigh an answer and look horizontally over the person's shoulder rather than up at the sky or down at the floor. But when you do this, keep your head level. Often an upward gaze looks like you're rolling your eyes, a downward gaze looks like you feel some level of shame, and an up and down gaze looks like you're checking out a pole dancer.

After looking over the shoulder, return to the person's head (that is not code for "get inside his or her head"). Add a "hmm . . . ah ha . . . I get it . . . tell me more . . . ," or give one slow deep nod but not bobble-head bounce.

You generally look at the person if you're doing the talking, so it's important to continue looking at the person when she's doing the talking. Otherwise, it will look like you think what she is saying is unimportant.

Now, if the person you are talking to nervously looks away, hold your focused look on her head or face so when she comes back, you're giving it to her again. If you look away as a reaction to her looking away, you look jittery.

Eyes that continually move away from the other person's face look distracted, shy, rude, or bored, or they can appear to be hiding something. Eyes that wander lasciviously about the person's body can get you sued.

Any direction other than horizontal looks less than "on the level." Remember, people read into your movement based on what their mom and dad taught them and what they learned watching television.

In some cultures and religions, it's respectful not to look in the dominant person's eyes. In others it's considered overbearing to give eye contact, and it's necessary to lower your eyes when speaking to a superior. You can respect cultural tradition, but you need to consider the message you send while doing it.

Speak Up to Be Seen and Heard

As much as I'm all for confidently and calmly listening with an open face and easy smile, there are times you must speak up to be seen and paid attention to. If what you have to say is worth saying, say it in a way that you get heard.

One CEO told me about a conversation he had with an employee, a middle-aged Asian man: "The employee told me, 'I was raised to speak when spoken to.' And I told him, 'You'll have to change that. You're here for one reason: to contribute.'"

You don't have to have Asian parents to have been taught that lesson: "Children are to be seen and not heard." "Speak when spoken to." These lessons have been preached in many households around the world. In the back of your head, you remember some coach or teacher saying something like, "Better to remain silent and thought a fool than to speak up and prove it."

Speak Up to Be Heard

When it is time for you to talk, make yourself effortless to be heard and easy to listen to. Eliminate from your speaking useless filler words that make you sound uncertain, unprepared, even uneducated: "you know ... uhm ... huh ... ah ... okay, okay ..." At the very least, if you must say them, say them silently to yourself when speaking out loud.

Research in the past has shown that people believe what they see over what you say. A recent study reported in the *Wall Street Journal* showed that people believe what you say based on *how* you say it at a two-to-one ratio.

Use a Level Voice

If you speak in an evenly modulated way without harshness, a lilt, or question at the end—with a consistent voice rhythm, timbre, and intonation—you sound authoritative. I call it a leveling "pass-the-salt" tone of voice. Even when very emotional around the dinner table, you typically speak a calm, clear, above-the-fray "pass the salt" as opposed to asking for the salt in an emotional outburst. One CEO told me, "Inside my head is a loud shrieking voice, but the outside knows to remain calm."

A level head, open mouth, and good posture all aid in your speaking voice because you open up your vocal apparatus by relaxing your jaw and throat, improving volume and projection. Direct your voice from your mouth to the listener's ears. Draw air from your diaphragm, not just your throat, so you project your words. A voice coach explained it to me this way: "Take the air from the room down inside of you."

She had us students do an exercise to hear the way we would sound if we were speaking from the diaphragm. Sit in a chair, spread your feet apart, place a magazine on the floor between your feet, bend over dropping your arms along the outside of your legs down toward your feet to force air out, and start to read out loud. You will hear what you are capable of if you breathe from the diaphragm and open up your throat. (Good places to practice diaphragm breathing and projection are when singing in the shower or singing along with the radio while sitting in traffic.)

Listen to messages you leave on voice mail to check your volume and rate of speaking and to hear if there is a smile in your voice. If people frequently ask you to repeat yourself, there is a good chance you talk too fast, you mumble, or you speak too low.

When your tonality is anything but an audible unemotional volume and pace, you can be read as insecure, angry, or fatigued. Likewise, mousy, shrill, thunderous, or brusque all trigger negative responses in people. Just as the face can show emotion that should or shouldn't be there, your voice definitely does too.

Voice coaches will tell you that a:

- Low voice is a dominance characteristic.
- Husky voice comes across as either powerful or scary.
- Fast, raised voice shows passion and conviction if heard and understood, but it also shows anxiety.
- Soft lead-in or wind-down can come off as weak.
- Harsh lead-in or wind-down can sound abrasive, arrogant, or out of control.
- Honeyed voice is flirtatious yet also soothing.
- Lower voice in women is more pleasing and powerful.
- Whisper, done in certain circumstances, is very loud.

If you're like me, you can't remember which tone to take on for which sentiment so it's best to have a consistent pass-the-salt quality.

When you're inconsistent, people don't believe you or trust you; and they worry about what might set you off emotionally next, so they simply avoid you. As one CEO told me: "I learned that when people bring you bad news and you scream and throw things at them, they won't bring you bad news again, and they probably won't bring good news either." Instead of varying your voice for your audience, you're better off to be constant, audible, and congenial to have your passion, conviction, and intensity steadily come through along with your choice of words.

A little variety in your speaking voice can still garner calm, confident, controlled communication. It's like a song: there is a faster, then a slower tempo, a variation of inflection and volume to make for enjoyable listening. You can similarly speed up or down, talk louder or quieter, all done on purpose for a purpose.

Whether it is a cowboy, an action hero, or a highly respected executive, a person in a position of power or with a strong demeanor doesn't say a lot. She doesn't have to because what she says has tremendous impact.

Stand Tall and Straight with Squared Shoulders and a Flat Back

Improving your posture is one of the quickest ways to differentiate yourself and come across as more confident in the workplace. As one CEO told me, "You either carry yourself like the hunter or the hunted." Just look around: few people are ramrod straight (and even fewer as they age).

Remember when I was giving physical descriptions used to describe character: "Levelheaded, head on straight, shifty eyed, can't look you in the eye"? Well, the ones for posture include "spineless," "gutless," and "with (or without) backbone."

Just reading the above causes a reflex reaction of sitting or standing better, right? So put that thought in your head 222 times a day as necessary. It's physical muscle development, just as you would use to increase your mental muscle. In a month you may have to remind yourself only 20 times a day, and in a year, 2 times, but you will always have to. One movie director was quoted as saying this: "I'd rather direct movies than act in them because when I direct, I don't have to stand up straight and pull my stomach in."

When you carry yourself with an air of easy command, you exude self-confidence and positive energy; you look youthful, healthy, and taller; and you present a better appearance, improve your voice, expand your breath airflow, align your internal organs, and take two inches off your waist.

Medical doctors will tell you that improved posture relieves chronic aches and pains, migraines, and sore neck and shoulder muscles; and it loosens stiff hips and a taut lower back. According to Dr. Vijay Vad, in his book *Back RX* (Gotham, 2004): "It fights the natural dehydration of the spinal column as you age and instead pumps a steady flow of oxygen to the discs. . . . When you do it, you yourself will experience it helping your core strength and enabling you to breathe more fully through your open chest."

Amy Cuddy, a Harvard researcher and social psychologist, did a 2012 TED Talk in which she discussed her findings that only two minutes of "power posing" (that is, a straight-up posture and open arms) increases your testosterone and decreases your cortisol. You look strong and seem taller.

In contrast, "slouching deepens depression, lowers your energy, brings about constipation because your intestines are folded, makes you look heavier, and ultimately causes career problems," writes Keely Savoic, in *Prevention Magazine* (November 2012).

From grade school on, we start hunching, rounding our shoulders when carrying backpacks, then come the laptops, and later in life, the diaper bags, the fashionable oversize purse, and inevitably, the "weight of the world." Stop it. You want to avoid being described as "He had the posture of a weary boxer" or "His shirt wasn't wrinkled, but he wore it like it was."

To be square shouldered and flat backed:

- *Lift your rib cage* up, away from your pelvis, raise your chest, but keep your chin parallel to the ground.
- *Roll back your shoulders, then pull them down.* "Imagine putting your right shoulder blade into your left back pocket and your left shoulder blade into your right back pocket," says Caroline Creagger, CEO of Executive Physical Therapies.
- *Pull your stomach in to your backbone.* Tighten your abdominal muscles, or as Creagger says, "Pull your belly button toward your spine, and keep breathing as you do it."

Other quick reminders to stimulate better posture:

- Imagine someone put an ice cube down your back.
- Think about how you fly a kite.
- Take a dance lesson.
- As strippers are taught, arch your back to present your body. (I know this one only from reading an article!)

As a little girl in church one day, I caught myself looking at my mother as she walked down the aisle to Communion. At that moment the thought crossed my mind, "She looks good. I'm proud she is my mom." She walked tall, and she looked happy and calm. A millisecond after that same moment, I overheard a nun sitting behind me comment to a fellow nun, "That Teresa Benton holds her head too high and walks too proud." It shook up my little 10-year-old brain a little because one authority figure, my mom, was walking with what looked good to me, but another authority figure, the nun, was disparaging toward her carriage and comportment. But as I've said before, a lot of things are in the eye of the beholder.

If for no other reason to do it, good posture might just keep you safer. Years ago researchers took video of people walking down the street into a prison and asked the inmates, "Whom would you choose to mug?" The overwhelming choice was the person with poor posture looking whipped, dejected, tired, old, feeble, and weak. That's one argument for good posture and a sure stride, but another is that it makes you appear taller, and taller people make more money in our society.

According to reporting on the *CBS Morning Show,* it's only an average of $789 per inch per year over the average height for either sex (the average male height is 5 feet 9 inches, and the average female height is 5 feet 4 inches)—but it's still something! Whatever height you are, hold yourself straight to make the most of it.

Anything that personally triggers you to stand, sit, and walk with good posture needs to be rechecked and recharged several times a day. Be flexible and move. It's not a rigidity that we're looking for. Stand tall. Carry yourself in a proud way. You'll set a good example for others, and you'll make them feel proud being around you. The late Congresswoman Shirley Chisholm used to say: "Hold your head up high—unbought, unbossed."

Slow Down

The more time you give yourself, the more status people give you. Move in haste but not in a hurry. A calm and slow demeanor will make you appear confident. Watch people whom you admire in public life, politics, and the corporate world, and notice how they move, stand, and hold themselves. You will not see rushed and hurried.

Fast is generally viewed as smug or worse, as nervous, seeking approval, or racing around the track to prove yourself.

Attorney Andrew R. Basile, Jr., of Young Basile, says: "A surprisingly common mistake young people make with executives or their clients is that they talk too fast and respond too quickly. It's probably borne of a fear that the busy executive will be unwilling to invest the time listening. Nothing could be further from the truth, but it telegraphs a message: 'What I have to say is not that important.'"

You can slow down physically but still continue to think fast. Just decelerate your physical deportment down a notch. When you do anything fast, you look like you are trying too hard to please.

Even though you are busy, brake and compose yourself once in a while. Now within reason, of course, you aren't walking down the office hallway the way you'd promenade down a church aisle to get married. But you should pause, not hurry and scurry, when you enter, exit, talk, walk, move, gesture, nod your head, answer, or speak up. Don't rush even when you scratch, push up your eyeglasses, or tug at your shirt sleeve.

Refrain and restrain yourself from impulse reaction. Be disciplined, be consistent, and keep at it despite the emotional pressure of the moment. "Let the flack pass." As one executive put it: "Think through what you want to do. . . . When you look and walk and talk and hold yourself in a certain way, everyone knows you're in charge—at least of yourself, and that's a start."

Carol Mithers wrote a piece called the "Benefits of Slowing Down" for the *Ladies' Homes Journal* (June 2010):

> Slow walking makes you more aware of your surroundings.
> Slow conversation makes for better interaction and connections.
> Slow eating makes you less likely to overeat.
> Slow spending helps you stay out of debt as you
> avoid the "see it, want it, buy it" impulse.
> Slow weight loss gives you the time to break bad habits.
> Slow hobbies helps you avoid mistakes when woodworking,
> sewing, knitting, painting, and so on.
> Slow sex is more fun (enough said).
> Slow parenting lets you enjoy raising your children.

There isn't much that doesn't benefit from your slowing down: walking, talking, texting, eating, spending, and judging others.

I was once answering questions about my company and research at a media event in France at the Paris Press Club to introduce my work to a European audience. Most of the French reporters in the audience spoke fluent English, but the press club provided a translator nonetheless. I caught myself expressing a thought with brief but succinct deliberation to make it easier for the interpreter to get my meaning, then I paused, and with an easy smile on my face, I looked at the audience as he translated. For an hour we did that dance: I spoke, paused, and patiently waited during the translation. At the end my assistant took me aside and said that it was the best presentation she had ever heard me deliver.

Replaying it in my head, I thought I sounded dumb speaking so slowly, but in fact, I was making it easier to be heard and understood. She told me later, "Sometimes you speak like you have a cheetah on your back," which was a very effective way of giving a critique to her boss!

People speed because it gives them the feeling they are manufacturing time for themselves. What happens in reality, however, is that they say or do something fast and realize only later the ramification. Automobile accidents and business accidents both come from speed. When you maintain an even pace, you avoid looking uncomfortable, and you steer clear of mistakes you probably wouldn't have made if haste hadn't been involved.

Remember, the secret to being cool, calm, collected, and confident is looking cool, calm, collected, and confident. All it takes is slowing down, standing straight, and keeping an easy smile on your face and in your head.

Clothes Can Be Purchased; Appearances Must Be Earned

I care less what you wear and more how you wear it. You can run into your boss at the grocery store on Saturday morning wearing a T-shirt and blue jeans and still look comfortable and confident if you smile, keep a level head, stand square-shouldered, and slow down.

A female fashion designer routinely on the annual international best-dressed list says this: "It is important to have a well-dressed mind." I was not in a position to ask her for the exact meaning of that statement, but my interpretation of her comment was that she was referring to how you differentiate your thinking as we discussed in Part I. Another fashion designer expressed his opinion this way: "To be well dressed, you have to be well naked." Again, my interpretation is that before clothes can help you in your presentation of your self, your physicality—that is, your posture, facial expression, eye contact, and pacing—must be aligned with the comportment of a confident, comfortable-in-your-own-skin, and competent person.

Clothes, like so much on the outside, are unfairly judged. I recall an audience member who came up to me after a Chamber of Commerce meeting where she was choosing speakers for upcoming events. She told me: "When I walked into the meeting room and saw you in that suit, I decided to walk out and go to a different speaker's presentation. I thought it was inappropriate. But I made my move to leave too late with the crowd coming in and the doors closing so I ended up staying, . . . and I'm sure glad I did. I learned more in this hour than in a 15-week course I took at the university last fall."

Now I decided to take it as a compliment that she enjoyed my presentation, but unfortunately there was no time at that moment to find out why my suit was "inappropriate" in the eye of this beholder. In hindsight, I wish I'd asked, "What about the suit caused your reaction: cut, color, style, fit, cost, . . . what?" In reality, it was a St. John, and it wasn't too short or too tight so I just forgot about it. But reflecting on it, I think that it was a lost opportunity for both her and me if she judged the inside by the outside dress. Still, people do it. Some people look at your shoes, your purse, your fingernails. They shouldn't, but they do—unfairly, unjustifiably, and undeniably. You and I do too, probably unconsciously if not consciously.

Fortunately it takes very little effort to wear suitable clothes to emulate successful businesspeople at the office. My few recommendations on your clothing are these:

- Have them fit your body, especially if you've gained or lost weight.
- Have items appear clean, without food particles or body odor.
- Have them be wrinkle free and not looking like they came from the bottom of the laundry basket. (You do not have to iron your underwear the way one executive's mother did in his youth.)
- And make sure your clothes aren't more interesting than you are. (If you aren't sure of my meaning, think Miley Cyrus.)

One CEO told me: "I dress one-third in the expected uniform of a CEO, one-third in fashion to please female employees, and one-third idiosyncratically to please myself," as he pointed to his ratty Yankees baseball cap hanging on the hat rack.

In the executive suite, I've seen others uniquely wear flowers in their lapels, pins to represent their mood, colorful socks, and wild ties. I even saw one CEO wear a rubber band around his wrist as a personal reminder of something dear to him. You can carry your own idiosyncrasy off if you combine it with good nature, good humor, comportment, and success in your field.

As I've written, I'm less concerned about what you wear than how you wear it in terms of posture and demeanor. Nonetheless, do not let casualness, ignorance, or sloppiness in dress be unnecessary hurdles you'll need to jump over. You can have your idiosyncratic doohickey, but make sure you've put the whole package together solidly otherwise.

Maintain an Effective Appearance

Try to adhere to the physical appearance recommendations in this chapter for 90 days. That is twice as long as the average New Year's resolution lasts, and it might be enough to start making it a permanent part of your lifestyle.

If you practice when it doesn't matter, you'll have a better chance of making it stick when it does matter. I am not recommending robot behavior and school uniform dress. I'm all for your uniqueness in how you express yourself. But I also know that there is much to think about, learn about, practice, and utilize in terms of actions far more important than appearance and physicality. So a little attention in this area can take you one step closer to another level as bosses see that you know how to fit in as well as stand out. You are a reflection of them, and if deportment is a nonissue, that's one more advantage for you.

It's forgivable if you've done any of this physically incorrectly in the past. It isn't if you continue doing it ineffectively.

CHAPTER 6

Be a Self-Starter

You're reading the wrong book if you have this attitude: "I don't want to be the first of anything new. I'll get all the sh**."

To differentiate yourself, be the one to initiate, not the one who waits. You cannot hesitate, waiting until you feel fully confident. You have to act on things now. You can't hold back on having an amiable temperament until the stars align and everything is all of a sudden going your way—it will never happen. You can't hold off on learning more because it's not immediately necessary. You can't wait for a good chance to make the first move. You have to be the example for others. You can't wait to be told what, why, when, or how to do things. You have to take the initiative to figure it out, trust your gut feeling, and take action.

CEOs tell me they want someone who:

- Is a self-starter.
- Initiates and doesn't wait.
- Is personally motivated.
- Has a can do–will do attitude.
- Does not procrastinate.
- Is proactive.
- Discerns what's missing.
- Goes toward something on her own.
- Doesn't need someone else to go first.
- Is an owner of anything that comes near him all the way to the final project.

The world is open to those who initiate doing more, differently and better. And as I've written before, it's not that difficult. Some examples of how some CEOs got a kick start in their career simply by instigating action:

- Wrote a letter to a U.S. president about a computer industry issue before it was widely discussed and got invited to present before Congress. Later was asked to head up the first presidential commission to deal with the issue.
- Took a stand arguing with the editor's position, defending her profession's reputation, and was asked to contribute a featured op-ed piece for the *Harvard Business Review*.
- Stepped up to the microphone when her boss got stage fright at the national association meeting and saved the presentation. Later got the boss's job.
- Walked up the 10 flights of stairs to a meeting instead of waiting for the elevator the way everyone else was. While singularly entering and later exiting the stairwell, was observed by an upper manager who introduced himself and said, "I'm supposed to take on a mentee this year. You're it."
- Had the nerve, while she was on vacation lounging by the pool in a swimsuit, to get up from the lounge chair and go talk to two executives from a prospective client company who were exiting from a meeting for a break and taking a stroll around the pool. Despite the unbusinesslike setting and attire, she didn't want to miss the opportunity to meet these two people who previously were not answering her phone calls. They later became her company's biggest clients.
- Set up an office in a new city by contracting a lease and furnishing the office in a two-hour time frame so as to satisfy a client's requirement to meet on site "this afternoon." The result was the signing of the biggest contract in the company's history.

None of those examples required permission from up above, an additional degree, a corporate pedigree, a high GPA, wealthy parents, or being 6 feet 4 inches with blond hair and blue eyes.

A self-starter mentality is imperative to CEOs. Taking the initiative shows you are a go-getter. If you need to be managed like a new hire and you wait until the boss brings you the latest task, you won't be viewed as having high potential. CEOs tell me this:

- "Ideas are a dime a dozen. Initiation and execution are worth everything."
- "Instead of ignoring a casual aside from a boss like 'I think it might be a good idea to . . .' because it means more work for you, jump on it. Climb all over anything the boss tells you to do. Carry through on the comment no matter how minor."
- "I don't have the time to give out new assignments. I want someone savvy enough to look around and see the priorities, where they should be spending their time. Their discernment shows that they understand the needs of the business and have a finger on the pulse of it, which impresses me."
- "What gets noticed by me? Self-initiative. Don't wait, and don't expect to be asked. Seek out work, come forth with ideas; speak about them with conviction."

You have hundreds of opportunities a month to take initiative (and at least 10 times today alone). It takes only seconds to start to do something greater, but it has ramifications for the rest of your career. You will grow in confidence, set yourself apart, get noticed, and likely make a significant difference in the organization, in your life, and in the lives of others.

Be the one who:

- Picks up the ball others have dropped.
- Volunteers first.
- Steps up to help out.
- Speaks up first.
- Takes it upon yourself to do more than asked or expected.
- Creates and innovates.
- Launches a new approach or idea.
- Lays the foundation for others to follow.
- Embarks, launches, or hatches a project or initiative.

I'm not for motion or activity to make it look like you work hard. I'm for real results that stem from your personal initiative to take on, step up, be first, or even be the only one to go beyond what's expected.

One CEO told me his trick is to take action in the first 10 minutes of coming up with an idea before self-doubt and questioning set in and build up and he changes his mind because, "Delay builds fear."

Don't wait for an attractive, juicy assignment. Be the self-started person who steps forward and doesn't wait to be asked—especially in undesirable areas. Take it upon yourself to even seek out the dirty work. Be willing to do something because it's hard, beneath you, and not what you were hired for. Instead of waiting for the high-profile assignments, spend time in the trenches doing the grunt work when necessary.

Seek assignments where you are needed most to achieve results toward your boss's mission. You can't be afraid of details and hesitant to get deep into hard work. You can't leave the detailed or mundane work to someone else. You do it.

One CEO put it this way: "When things are hard, work three times harder if you want to be different and stand out."

You be the one who knows what's going on, gets involved with the unpleasant or boring parts, follows through, and gets the job done. And while you're at it, instead of pressuring your boss for an expanded budget, initiate cost reductions in your department. Ask for a leaner, tighter budget.

After you take the initiative, follow through all the way to the finishing point—specifically, the finishing point that the boss wants. What you think is completed work may not be what your boss had in mind. Check with her. Don't guess or assume. You would think this idea is a given, but it isn't. Most people believe they give full-out effort, but this thought is one that is in the eye of the beholder. Even if they go for a codified 100 percent, you'll almost never see 110 percent. Contributing 100 percent plus 10 percent more toward what the boss wants is a huge differentiator, "a superseparator on steroids," as one leader put it. Putting 110 percent toward the *wrong* objective isn't.

The work that constitutes 100 percent is in the eye of the beholder (like a lot of things we've discussed), and it varies among different tasks, in different areas, with different people. And though it may seem extreme, keep in mind Ernest Hemingway's advice: "Always do sober what you said you'd do drunk"—by which he meant, stick to your word and follow through on it.

Instead of doing work to your satisfaction, sometimes the best thing is to do it to the satisfaction of those you are doing it for. Don't leave a job until it's complete enough in their eyes. Bosses hate it when they have to remind you to conclude a task. Don't be the person who has to be followed and checked up on to finish the last 5 percent of the job.

Is it important to get to 100 percent always? Sometimes it's better to get eight things done at 90 percent than four things at 100 percent. As I wrote earlier, find out the expectations of your boss and meet them. Sometimes you end up doing the wrong thing if you go "full out" when the situation, timing, circumstances, and people involved don't require it. In such cases, doing more isn't adding value. It's such a fast-paced, on-demand world that sometimes getting things done at 42 percent is the best that time will allow. What becomes a separator is not doing 110 percent but being the initiator, the self-starter.

Dino Falaschetti, executive director of PERC, told me this:

> When I was at the White House as a senior economist for the Council of Economic Advisors, we were given an initial briefing to understand how Washington works versus business. We were told if it's 80 percent done, make a decision and go on to the next thing. We have too many things to do. . . . We'd get the president's or secretary of state's speeches in advance for fact checking. One speech on Katrina was totally wrong, but all I had time to do was change the worst paragraph. I did, and that paragraph ended up on the front page of the *Wall Street Journal*. But it certainly wasn't what I would have liked to have done in terms of doing the job 100 percent.

You have to initiate for magnificent things to happen. When you've stretched yourself that way, it is so rewarding to look back on something you've done that at one time you thought you never could.

CHAPTER 7

Pour Your Heart
into Your Art

YOU HAVE to passionately want to differentiate yourself from others. You must be inflamed about this idea. Not just because I want it for you but because you can't imagine doing *anything* but going for it.

The shocking, surprising, and sad fact is that few people do have fire in their belly from passion and curiosity. There are many reasons why:

- They don't want the stress of success.
- They are comfortable where they are, and they don't want to change their work, geographic location, colleagues, or much of anything else.
- They don't want to have big goals only to fall short.
- None of their friends or family members are striving for more and better.
- They don't think they are worthy or good enough. They think they are too young, too old, and too heavy, they are in the wrong function, or they have an inappropriate work pedigree.
- They are afraid that people will think that they think they are special.
- They tried once, it didn't work, and they don't want to try again.
- They don't want to work long, hard hours. They are satisfied with doing whatever is minimally necessary.
- They were told that people who make it to the top are thieves.
- They are scared.
- They have lost their ambition to do anything but tread water.
- They don't know what to do next.

If you have any of those unhelpful thoughts, you need to put them into your mental paper shredder. They do not support where you're going in life. They might have come from your mom and dad or from some actual experiences, but you have to put a stop to them; otherwise, they will drain your energy. If instead, you get excited about doing whatever you are doing, you will get a sort of energy that puts you on an entirely different level than every other human being.

In reality, you really have two ways to go:

1. Love what you're doing.
2. Love the doing.

Love the Doing

"Loving what you're doing" means you are fortunate enough to be making a living in the arena of your choosing. Pro golfers come to mind, as do most any other professional athletes. These people have gotten so good at their obsession that they get to earn money for doing it.

Despite our weekend warrior talent, few of us will ever stand apart from our competitors enough to make it a career the way Danica Patrick, Peyton Manning, Vjah Singh, Laird Hamilton, Tony Hawk, and Antonio Silva have.

"Loving the doing" means that regardless of your current title, function, or industry, you toil to always do whatever you do, differently and better than the rest.

CEOs tell me this:

- "I want individuals who don't let colleagues, relatives, friends, society, pessimists, guilt, fear, or ignorance stand between them and their goals."
- "If you can't figure out how to make it fun, it's your problem."
- "People talk about the golden pot at the end of the rainbow. But I want people who see that the whole rainbow is nice."
- "One of my top employees said to me once, 'I do my best, and in God I trust the rest. . . . I don't have to climb to the moon to feel accomplishment. I just stay enthused about the task at hand.'"

Finding some unique, even idiosyncratic interest and turning it into a prosperous career can happen—with work, luck, and timing. Look at the Robertson family from the TV show *Duck Dynasty*, who started making duck calls along with their fishing business activities and turned the combined enterprises into a multimillion-dollar operation. The company now manufactures the original duck calls, to which it has added buck calls. What's more, the *Duck Dynasty* trademark is now affixed to hats, hunting clothing, T-shirts, cups, beer mugs, and more. The company even has a book publishing and speaking franchise too.

A similar success is John Bianchi. While he was a police officer in New York, he spent his spare time making holsters by hand for his service weapon. He is left-handed, and up until he invented the design for himself, left-handers were handicapped with their holsters. His six carefully crafted, handmade prototypes—and complete inventory—were stolen while they were drying behind his house one evening. It was his passion, so naturally he started over on another six. To make a long story short, he continued until he left the police force, moved to California, and started a company that ended up becoming the largest manufacturer of police and military holsters in the world.

One entrepreneur spoke with glee as he told me about his small manufacturing company where he made fake severed fingers that looked like they had been cut off by a knife in a bar fight. He told me with great pride, "They are so authentic-looking that a few times they've ended up in crime labs as evidence."

If you get to work in your sport, craft, art, or idiosyncratic calling, that's absolutely great and fortunate, but most of us won't. Therefore, our option is to love the doing. Everything in this book supports option 2 because in reality, that is where most people are in their professional career.

Here is one CEO's backstory of working in that manner. After graduating from college with plans to be an investment banker, the man couldn't get a job in the rough economy so he started driving cabs, soon moving up to limos. He was taking a passenger he had picked up in Midtown Manhattan, New York City, to LaGuardia Airport, but they'd had a late start, and traffic was heavy. The panicked passenger was bemoaning missing his flight. The limo driver took it upon himself to check other airlines' schedules for a flight out of JFK International and Newark International to the same destination but at a manageable time. The driver's research discovered a doable flight out of JFK, so he sped off in that direction. The late and harried passenger didn't have time to pay as he jumped out and raced to the gate. The limo driver handed him his card saying, "Don't worry about it. Just get going. Here is my address, and you can pay me when you get home." Turned out the passenger had just been named a senior executive of Credit Suisse. He and the driver had so much time to talk during the race to the airports that he learned about the driver's background and avid interest in investment banking. And very important, he saw a demonstration of the driver's initiative and resourcefulness. The driver practiced "love the doing" and worked with dedication even though it wasn't his "passion." Along with the fare payment—four times what was due—came an invitation for a job interview that led to an offer in investment banking that over the years has progressed into an extremely high-profile and profitable career.

So don't wait for the perfect situation to come along before you get that unquenchable lust for what you're job is. It's great if your work and "love" fit like a lock and key. But if they don't, have "love the doing" be your art.

Seek excellence in the execution of the job at hand regardless of whether you work for a waste treatment plant, a herpes medication company, or even a politician.

CEOs tell me that they want people:

- Who are full of ambition and goals.
- Who sing—well, silently hum—at work.
- Who stretch themselves every day and who always have new challenges they're hankering to take on.
- Who get an emotional kick out of any accomplishment.
- Who are juiced (in the nonsteroid way) every morning to get out of bed and go for it.

- Are hungry (figuratively).
- Are afraid of *not* fulfilling their destiny.

It's up to you to start and kindle the fire in you. No one can do it for you. A spouse might push you, a boss who sees potential might press you, a life-changing situation (divorce, death of someone close, job termination, birth of a child, or something else) might prompt a flicker. As is true of any fire, whatever ignition you start with will fizzle out if you don't continuously feed the fire.

Even working in your passion gets boring. Rock stars get tired of groupies; circus performers get worn out picking up elephant dung; and pro football players get weary of sitting in ice baths after the games to help heal sore muscles. The late Malcolm Forbes wrote: "If you have a job that lacks being tedious, boring, occasionally inconsequential, and aggravating, you don't have a job."

If you "check out" in any way, you weigh the whole team down—and you leave yourself behind.

Be Consistent and Relentless

For your passion to "take," the mindset, comportment, and behavior you choose have to be predictable, reliable, and repeatedly consistent all the time. People up, down, and around are watching to decide if they can depend on you and your actions. They monitor, scrutinize, and even mimic your moves. If you are sporadic and random in your actions, you will not be justifiably authentic and genuine. If people don't know what to expect or what they can count on, they won't have faith in, or trust, you.

Be Consistent

You differentiate yourself when you do what you do on your best day, every day. Routine reduces stress—yours and that of those around you. Successful outcomes happen from tenacious consistency whether it is toward your business goals or your golf game.

Pros are consistent; amateurs are inconsistent.

Sure, you can distinguish yourself with a one-time stunt or gimmick, but then you're only a one-trick pony. You need to differentiate yourself with positive predictability over time, sustained over the long term. Being steady does not mean you won't or can't change; it doesn't mean you are overly pliant; and it doesn't mean you are obstinate. It means being reliable, dependable, and unfailing in your conduct, which, by the way, becomes your character.

Without constancy, your genius will be wasted.

CAUTION: ENVY WILL REAR ITS UGLY HEAD

A caution about your pouring your heart into your art: it will spark jealousy.

Surprisingly one of the toughest parts of success is finding a colleague happy for you. But as they say, "Anyone can get pity. Jealousy you have to earn."

Following the advice in this book might cause you some trouble. When you persistently do off-the-charts good work, the unintended consequence is that you make other people look bad. That can create a problem for you because frankly, people are often envious of your effort and success. It's crazy, but you will be reviled by some for your exertion. They are afraid you'll make them look inferior—their worst fear. I've asked many CEOs what was the biggest surprise they experienced once becoming CEO, and the majority told me some version of being taken aback by how many enemies they then had.

One told me that it is a double-edged sword to differentiate yourself:

When you get noticed, get rewarded, get recognition, coworkers, family, and friends can turn on you. Jealousy is a unique human instinct, and it can create a divide. Instead of lauding your accomplishments, they make snide remarks. I remember my coworkers griping, "You're making us all look bad," and then reacting by trying to make me look bad. It was a total surprise to me that that would happen.

People are jealous because you remind them of their weaknesses, which makes them feel fearful and insecure. When you are a nobody, doing nothing, no one cares. But if you start leading the pack, you'll get the arrows in your rear. That's just life.

This caution is not to suggest that you rein in your effort to differentiate. Being passionate, consistent, and to be relentless is not to be a show-off or to try to prove how great you are.

The only thing you can do is to try in every way to highlight and spotlight the accomplishments of others. When they do well, praise and laud them. Do not hold back praise or retaliate against them in any way. Just continue to pour your heart into your craft. And in a private place on your body, you can tattoo in Sanskrit: "Success is the best revenge."

Be Relentless

Tenacity yields a big payback for a small effort. Persistent people just get started when others cave in and give up.

If you are willing to consistently persevere, no person, outside force, current circumstance, or future obstacle can keep you from your destiny. If that means following up with some opportunity 4 times or 14, you need to do it. Now, you also need not be tedious, irritating, or bothersome, but you can be creative. Author Katy Pitrowski told me about getting her first professional writing gig by phoning a man every week for four weeks—always with a new angle or idea—until one day when he answered, he simply said, "You're hired." The successful entrepreneur John Bianchi, whom I mentioned earlier, stated in his book *An American Legend*, "Nothing ever happens with one attempt." Experts in skill development say it takes 10,000 hours of practice in a specific area to truly be good. Now that's a lot of determination!

The truth is that persistence and drive override skill. When people say "no," it's a "no" for now. It doesn't mean you can't or shouldn't come back with a new approach. One CEO told me, "I always give 'no' as the first answer, and only if they don't give up but have the confidence to persist and come back at me will I believe their conviction."

Being a self-starter is the same as being the last to quit, give up, give in, and sign off. Nothing ever happens unless one initiates and keeps trying what was started—with creativity that comes from continuous learning to give you new ideas and approaches.

There will always be endless reasons to cave in "this one time" because you are tired, sick, mad, put down, challenged, threatened, beaten, or bullied—or whatever other reason you give yourself. *Stick to it*. Don't give up, walk away, or abdicate your promise to yourself.

When you try something that doesn't work, try it again, in a new way, and if that doesn't work, try another new way. There is seldom one right answer. The only truly wrong answer is no attempt. It's ironic that the more you persist, the more strength you acquire to keep going at it and trying again. Don't give yourself excuses or exceptions.

Henry Ward Beecher, twentieth-century American clergyman and lecturer, wrote: "The difference between perseverance and obstinacy is that one often comes from a strong will and the other from a strong won't."

The biggest reason for consistency and persistence is to avoid being a moving target—in other words, being one personality to one person, another to someone else. Be a known quantity. Pick your style, and stick to it. If you are a moving target, you frustrate people, and you create ambiguity, uncertainty, and divisiveness in the organization. People don't know how, when, why, where, and what to do with you.

You become guilty of playing office politics when you set different standards for different people—people will think, "Why does he get this and I don't get it?" Instead, be consistent in giving people what you want them to see, absorb, and respond to.

Tolerate nothing that keeps you from your goal of doing more and doing it better in your good work. Nag yourself to stick with it until or unless you get additional information that causes you to change course.

Nothing in this book differentiates you if you don't stick to it in a patient and focused manner. Giving up or giving in is the most common impediment to career success.

Regardless of anything in your past, going forward is what you choose for it to be. Don't cut corners on yourself—you're too valuable.

PART III

How to Differentiate Your Actions

CHAPTER 8

Do a Stellar Job

EVERYTHING IN this book is for naught if you don't get the job that you are paid to do successfully completed—*and more*. It doesn't impress bosses at all if you just do what is required.

Stellar work is your personal wealth: your worldly goods, trust fund, gold stash, life preserver, money in your pocket, and 401(k). It is the investment in yourself that no one can take away and no depressed economy or down market can diminish.

"In the football world, it's called making plays. Everyone in the game is fast, big, and strong, but only a certain percentage can make the big plays week in and week out," says Steven Israel, retired NFL player for the Carolina Panthers and now the CEO of EndZone Coverage.

So what does "stellar work" mean to the CEOs I asked? You should:

- Make your numbers and deliver results on time, within budget.
- Know the most important areas to focus on, and you make them better.
- Find a need and fill it as well as you can.
- Make your boss's life more comfortable and easier.
- Make your boss look good. You never surprise her, and you always keep her in the loop.
- Are willing and flexible to take on more when asked, and better yet, you discover openings before being asked.
- Have your work complement others' work. You do what you can to help groups outside of your immediate job area.
- Do damn fine work, and you are a damn fine person.
- Do things that seem impossible to do.

- Deliver faster, cheaper, with higher quality.
- Are the fulcrum mover.
- Extract the most from an opportunity.
- Act as eyes and ears with the goal of improving the company's achievements outside of your immediate job area.
- Utilize a broad and diverse set of skills—that is, you are multidisciplined.
- Can track your successful history of making good decisions with value-added contributions.
- Deal with complex tasks without needing your handheld.
- Make it fun with the right amount of friskiness and playfulness in getting along and making things happen.
- Always look at how other people are doing the same type of work you're doing. You always try to find people who are better at it and studying what they are doing.
- Figure out how to fix what is thrown at you.
- Think like an owner. You promote the organization's mission, not just your own.

Two more colorful answers: "Work like a rented mule" and "To do a good job nowadays, you just need to be sober, honest, and bathe."

Kidding aside, when your boss gives you assignments, recognize that you will be viewed as "pretty good" if you do what's expected. But that's not good enough. As one CEO explained his thinking early in his career, "I discovered that if I met my boss's expectations, out of the roughly 100 people that I was competing with, I'd end up in a group of 10 who got favorably noticed. And if I could put a spin on things that caused my boss to say, 'Wow, that's great, I never thought of doing that,' instead of a group of 10, there would be only 1 or 2 who did that."

Good work is done with sincere intent, not political intent. You don't do it to impress but to demonstrate what you can do.

You'll find a couple of things are likely to happen when you exert yourself in that manner. First, you'll likely stimulate the intellectual thought and activity of other people around you, and second, the boss will probably give you bigger and more important projects.

As one CEO told me, "The secret is to get assigned things where there is little assurance that it will work. But the boss figures if anyone can get it done, you can because of your track record. That's where your real opportunity lies."

If early on, or at the latest midcareer, you put your trademark on a few meaty problem assignments in this manner, it will set you up for the rest of your career life.

Solve More Problems Sooner and Better Than Other People Do

You are in your job for one reason: to solve problems.

Business life is made of problems—and thank goodness for that! Troubles truly are opportunities. They're the vehicles for learning, growing, and proving yourself on the job. The good thing is that the sooner you conquer one difficulty, you free yourself up to proceed to the next one.

In reality, a job is a to-do list and game plan interrupted by problems. Few days unfold trouble free. A phone message or e-mail brings an unplanned-for, unanticipated crisis. While dealing with that issue, another message or a colleague comes in with another new dilemma. It goes on incessantly throughout the day and into the next.

Every day things go wrong. Doing a stellar job means you fix them.

Problems range in size and intensity, but generally speaking anytime you have a difference between what you have and what you want, it's a problem. And it needs to be dealt with in an analytical, thorough, and logical approach. Don't be caught off guard by incessant tribulations. Assume something will go wrong today.

This is not negative thinking, it's preemptive. If you anticipate the possibility you won't be stunned and caught off guard. Ask yourself, "What could happen to mess this up?" If you don't consistently pose that question, you aren't doing the complete job.

Count on the probability that the worst thing will always happen at the worst time. If you expect things to get messy, by anticipatory thinking and action, you can keep them from getting messier.

In fact, if you want to be known as achieving results in business, pray for tricky, insipient, wicked problems for yourself. One Washington politician admitted in a private conversation that he always made whatever problem presented look more difficult than it really was so he would look like a hero when he solved it. (No surprise in U.S. politics, right?)

Not all problems will be career changing. Some will just be flat-out tedious, but they still need to be solved. As one CEO said to me, consider the problems as "the salt you put on food because without the salt, the food would be boring."

When presented with a problem, a good first reaction bosses like to hear is some version of: "I'm on it." "No problem." "Consider it done." A puzzled, confused gaze of perplexity should be camouflaged.

Understand and define the problem. Albert Einstein once said, "If I had an hour to solve a problem, I'd spend 55 minutes thinking about the problem and 5 minutes thinking about solutions."

It helps to think about a problem from the perspective of all people involved.

Say a water main breaks that forms a sink hole on a city street. Commuters late to work are frustrated and irritated, and they pass those feelings along as road rage. Police and fire departments take extra safety precautions, causing more delay for the commuters and others. The local news agency gets to send the rookie reporter out on breaking news. Now instead of sitting at her desk texting, the rookie reporter gets her shot at airtime. Her mother takes to Facebook and Twitter to brag. Since there is water damage on the cars in the streets, repair shops prepare for a bump in business. Insurance companies gear up for flood damage claims. The city maintenance crews who inspected the pipe last week worry about their job security and even legal liability. The lawyers anticipate the lawsuits. Kids are happy because they can't go to school. The pest control people gear up for rodent removal. The city council members call for an emergency debate on the city's infrastructure plans. Candidates for the upcoming city council election seize the vulnerability and change their speech for the Optimists' lunch. The water pipe manufacturers scurry to get the right gauge in inventory.

Long-haul truck drivers get to pick up unplanned loads, bringing in extra money for their kids' braces. The ducks get a new pool to paddle around in, at least for the day.

My point: a seemingly small problem can have so many dimensions that many other people experience the ramifications beyond your initial evaluation of the situation. Doing a stellar job means the whole job in the eyes of others involved, not just your part. It's a version of doing 110 percent versus 100 percent.

Problems have a lot of dimensions so it helps in your decision making to ask questions and consider the perspectives of the wide range of people involved—the externalities. Doing so will help you come up with an analytical, thorough, and logical resolution. Ask questions like these:

- What is the problem in total?
- Who thinks so?
- What has been tried?
- Who has tried it?
- What was their outcome?
- Why is it happening now?
- And most any other question that starts with who, what, when, why, or where.

Sort out the facts from the opinions that you get. Remove your own feelings as much as you can. Break the issues into attackable, doable parts instead of trying to tackle them all in one fell swoop. Remove any bottlenecks you can.

Write down all the possible options because you elaborate, concentrate, and evaluate more objectively in print than you can just in your head. Weigh the choices; mull over the plusses and minuses. Pull the best solutions from the list. Test them if you can. Contemplate the consequences of both the solutions you chose and those you didn't choose. Decide on which are feasible. Keep asking, "What could mess this up?"

Occasionally step away, get a clear head, regroup, and go back in at a different angle when you re-engage. Set a deadline for each step;

it will cause you and others to scramble. Have a plan B if things prove to not be wholly solvable. Present recommendations or resolutions in a concise, clear manner. Stand on them unless or until additional information causes you to change your mind.

If you wait until you can do no wrong in solving the problem, you'll wait forever. Nothing will ever get done. Expect potential or additional problems to pop up around your decisions. Remind yourself that your ability to deal with, overcome, solve, go around, and eliminate is your job—and it's what makes work life interesting. And the sooner you solve one problem, the sooner you can go onto the next one.

Most important, don't take problems to your boss. Take solutions. Why let him have all the fun?

The business problem-solving techniques you hone will carry over to your personal life. Some CEOs relayed to me stories of preventing potential personal predicaments by following the advice one EVP gave me: "Correct the problems before they occur." That strategy was evident in many stories CEOs told me:

- One CEO who had inherited his father's financially prosperous company told me about removing DNA samples of his dad's hair at the mortuary. "My father was quite the ladies man, and I wanted to arm myself with evidence against any woman's claiming paternity rights."
- Another had his future wife and him go to a psychiatrist and take compatibility tests. He also had his close friends do assessments and evaluations on both of them separately and as a couple—all in hopes of avoiding a later divorce.
- Yet another wealthy CEO circumvented having to ask his fiancée for a passion-cooling prenup by arranging his finances, with the fiancée's knowledge, in such a manner that if divorced, money went to a third party, and neither could touch it. He did sweeten the arrangement by putting a million dollars in her account for every year of their marriage, and at last count it was 25!

Do More, and Do It Better

Instead of trying to get comfortable in your job, try to get constantly *un*comfortable. Seek out problems, look for potentially painful experiences, approach the scariest people, juggle more balls than most people handle, and put an extra percentage of "umph" into everything you do.

You will likely find that you can do what you never thought you could. Here are some CEOs' versions of doing more early on in their careers:

- "I specifically looked for work in areas where there was no competition—or slothful, stupid competition."
- "To stand out from my competitors, I always offered to work for a month for free, and at the end of it, if I liked the organization and they liked my work, it was a win-win situation for both."
- "I discovered that standing out from the crowd is not about putting in an extraordinary effort on a single task, or a single job, or on a single day. It is simply doing the little things that others aren't willing to do . . . and not just when you feel like doing them but the whole time."
- "It's trite, but I try to be more informed, work harder, quicker, and hopefully smarter than my peers . . . and with no higher priority than to solve problems."

If you are in sales, sell more to more people while spending less on expenses, and help your fellow salespeople do the same. If you are in finance, figure out ways to save the company money as well as increase revenues and worth. Share what you're doing with colleagues to assist them in doing the same. If you are in IT, make information more accessible, usable, and faster across the board, and lend a hand to the nontechie types to make the technology easier for them. If you are in marketing, creatively get more positive exposure for the organization to support sales, and be inclusive of other departments' goals too. And if you are in human resources, resolve issues quicker, get processes in place, and communicate among all levels more efficiently and effectively so all have buy-in.

When TJ Walker's book came out, *TJ Walker's Secret to Foolproof Presentations* (Greenleaf Book Group Press, 2009), he wanted to do more to promote it. He set a goal to conduct a record number of talk show interviews in a 24-hour period. With massive behind-the-scenes organization culminating in the daylong event, he succeeded in getting 112 talk show interviews scheduled. It literally qualified him for the *Guinness Book of Records*, which brought another wave of publicity. He said it was physically grueling to stay awake for 24 hours, but his book ended up at number one on the bestseller lists for *USA Today*, *Businessweek*, and the *Wall Street Journal*.

If work opportunities aren't coming fast enough, go find them. If you risk and fail, you're still further ahead in learning than those who didn't try.

When you "do more," make sure it's what management wants and needs. Keep your boss in the loop. It's unproductive to do more when it's something she doesn't want done.

One CEO told me the story of assigning the task of creating an advertising kiosk for an industry convention. The engineer took on the assignment with such vigor that he ended up with an electronic, motorized, digitalized booth that was so big it required a Mack truck to transport it to the site. It turned out to be too unwieldy, wide, and expensive, and ultimately it was unusable. "It was engineered to the *n*th degree, and 'doing more' in this case was a mistake on the engineer's part," said the CEO.

One sales VP told me the story about flying across the country to save a customer relationsip—a customer he later found out the company was hoping to drop.

Don't jump on or jump into someone else's turf even with good intent. Communicate with the people involved, and ask lots and lots questions. No detail is too small to learn about if it matters to your boss or the team.

Doing more involves building good work upon good work. So if you do 90 percent of a job today, tomorrow you start from that 90 percent point. But if you got to a 100 percent or, better yet, 110 percent today, that's where you start off tomorrow. You build exponentially, and that is a huge differentiator, always being steps ahead of others in the same time frame.

At all times think about how you can do your job better, provide more value, and expand your impact on the organization—within the realm of what is needed and wanted. Don't storm in telling the CEO or other leaders what you want to do. Solicit what their needs are around the situation:

- Instead of saying out loud or even in your head, "That's not my job," you say, "What can I do to help?"
- When you see a need in someone else's turf, go to the person and ask questions such as these:
  - "I see a need in _____. I think I could do _____. Would that be of help?"
  - "I was wondering if I could lend a hand in _____. I could contribute by _____."
  - "I have an interest in _____. Is there some way I can be of assistance? You can talk to _____ and see what I've been doing around this kind of project that could benefit you."
- When an idea is suggested that means extra work for you, say, "Can I take a shot at that?"

Kevin Willis, CFO of Ashland, told me about an experience early in his career. He got a call from his boss at 10:30 one evening. "You want to go to Europe to work?" he asked. Kevin answered, "When do you need to know?" His boss responded, "Now." Kevin said, "Okay." He told me, "My whole career I had happily chosen to take on what others wouldn't do as quickly. I'd raise my hand and volunteer to go to Nigeria if I had to. I'd schlep around anywhere in the world. I don't mind change, and I don't mind ambiguity."

To differentiate: do more and do better, you'll find that it's not that difficult. Think about everything I have written:

- You set yourself apart from other good performers when you display more confidence, more often. It's not that difficult to act it, particularly when you take on some of the physicality expected of a confident person: stand tall, pace yourself, and look comfortable in your own skin.
- Honesty removes the burden of having to remember lies.
- Being good-natured makes it easier for people to work with you.
- You more easily come up with new ideas when you stay curious, always clamoring to learn more about people, places, and things.
- It's more fun and easier being the initiator of a project than having to be the follower. One CEO described his entrepreneurial attitude this way: "I decided that if I wanted to be the head of my profession, I'd have to create my profession."
- It's easy to go to work when you love what you do or you choose to love the doing. You end up as Warren Buffett is famous for saying he does, "singing on his way to work."

In the following chapters, you'll see that it's not that difficult to differentiate yourself in your risk-taking ability, communication manner, and helping others do well. That being said, as uncomplicated as I try to make it, the big separator is still being the one who actually turns up the all-out effort in executing this advice on a consistent basis. You don't have to go back to school, dye your hair, lose weight, or move to a different company or city. Right here, right now, you can go beyond what you'd normally do and go beyond what others do.

CHAPTER 9

Take Calculated Risks

THERE IS a saying among old cowboys out West: "One man with courage is the majority."

When I write about courage, intestinal fortitude, guts, and boldness to differentiate yourself, it's not to encourage you to do stupid, risky things. I'm not looking for the daredevil mentality that causes you to rappel off the Brooklyn Bridge or swim with the sharks. Nor need you be as daring as one CEO who said: "I've always taken chances. At 54 years old, I married an 18-year-old. Her dad didn't like me or the idea at all. I told him, 'Look, you're not losing a daughter. You're gaining a brother.' . . . I was a hyper child, always getting into trouble like the time I looked inside a gas tank with a match. I learned you don't do that."

I'm not asking for utter fearlessness and risk without thinking. Just "go for it" a little more and more often than you have in the past—and more often than others do. If you hold back, you'll get into a rut, slip behind, fade out of sight, and sink into the sameness of the people around you.

A calculated risk is just another way of saying:

- Show some spine.
- Put it on the line and see it through.
- Leave it all on the playing field.
- Creatively work with fear.
- Think the unpopular thing.
- Have the gumption to go off the grid.
- Be willing to bet your job on a hunch.
- Step out of the box.
- Be unafraid to fall flat on your face.

If you don't fight through timidity, you will have regrets. Few individuals look back on their lives and think, "Wow, I should have never tried for that bigger job." But many will look back with regret: "Why didn't I have the guts to try for that bigger job?" Or "Why didn't I speak up?" "Why didn't I step up?" "Why didn't I step it up?" "Why . . . why . . . why?"

Being scared is one of the strongest driving forces in life: scared of being talked about, laughed at, and pitied. One CEO told me, "Ironically, being scared gave me courage. . . . I never wanted to take on a job if there wasn't fear. I try to teach my mentees, don't bite off less than you can chew."

Everything is a risk/reward trade-off. The higher the chance you take, the bigger the price. Measure caution and daring to find a balance you can live with at this point—then push past that point going forward.

Don't wait for permission or even encouragement. Ignore the voice that tells you to turn around and shirk away, disregard what others might think of you, and accept that it's okay to be afraid but to act anyway. Forget the pain of past missteps. Things will be daunting, but don't let that stop you. Your action isn't big enough if it doesn't scare you. So find what scares you, then go do that. Go to whatever is your imaginary edge, and step across it. Go out on a limb more than you want or is required.

It's a mistake to think if you have courage in one area of life, then you have it in all areas. Most people are brave only in situations they have exposed themselves to. So expose yourself to the most experiences, people, and places that you can.

The more frequently you put yourself into uncomfortable and difficult situations, the less often you will find yourself in situations in which you will have had no experience. Don't let your long series of successes get stalled before you take on your first difficult challenge. A great deal of opportunity is lost in the business world for want of a little courage.

Use your smarts, think things through, prepare for alternatives, plan your steps, and all the while consider the danger. I'm not asking you to take action that will cause you to have to look for another job.

A gamble needn't be outrageous. It can be a gentle pushback, standing your ground, and expecting acceptance and doing what you can to get it. Little victories regularly are as important as big ones periodically. They become favorite "moments" to look back on—and add to your life story!

This is not an earth-shaking example but a real-life, day-to-day type of experience that you and I deal with.

When I was young, unknown, with few credentials, I had to stand up for myself against a behemoth businessman when I could have easily shirked away.

I had worked for three months to get an in-person appointment with a media mogul CEO to land a chance to introduce my company and potentially propose some consulting services to him. He was the biggest player in the industry, and he was reputably the most difficult to get an appointment with. Through tenaciously making nearly 20 attempts in various ways to get to talk to him, and with a little luck from someone else's personally recommending to him that he should see me, I finally got a one-hour appointment: 8 a.m., two months out.

The morning of the meeting, his secretary called and postponed it to 10 a.m. It caused me to shuffle my schedule and change my return flight home at the last minute at an extra cost, but I decided he was too important not to do it.

So I showed up at 9:50 after prepping my pitch and selecting the perfect outfit (I'd heard appearances were extra important to this person, as he was the type that had male manicures), and I was geared up to meet him. I waited and waited outside his executive office. By 11:05, there still was no explanation or apology from him or his secretary. I noticed a management type was there also. I asked, "Are you here to see Mr.__?"

"Yes, I have a 10:00 appointment," he said, a little disgusted for having to wait the way I was.

Well, I had to wait, too, and after a lot of effort! When I learned that the man had an appointment at the same time as mine, I could see what was going to happen—the secretary would likely defer to him. So at 11:06, I casually found a reason to be up off the reception area sofa and on my feet, nonchalantly stepping away from the sitting area with the excuse to politely make a phone call out of earshot. What I was doing was putting myself inches closer to what I figured was the CEO's inner sanctum. Finally, at 11:24, the secretary entered the reception area to collect the man with the 10:00 appointment. I smiled at her with the firm pronouncement, "I have a 10:00 with Mr._." By the time the man with the other appointment stood up, I was halfway in the CEO's office and not stopping.

Once in, the CEO did not stand up to shake hands. He kept his head down and continued with some papers on his desk, just motioning for me to sit down. But I didn't sit down. I waited until he seemed to pause. When he finally looked up at me, he looked as though he was wondering why I hadn't obeyed him.

There was a silence as both of us waited for the other to speak. Finally, with a calm voice and a relaxed smile on my face, I gently chided, "This appointment isn't very important to you, is it?" He looked at me as if he was considering suggesting that I leave. Instead, he put his pen down, pushed his chair back, and said with a half-smile, "Let's see if you can make it important to me." And I did. He became a client.

Months later he said to me, "You took a big risk coming on like that. But it's the only reason I let you continue."

My friend Sandra Walston, business consultant and author of the book *Courage*, told me about a situation early in her career as an entry-level business development officer for a bank in West Los Angeles:

My job responsibilities consisted of qualifying profitable clients in the bank's target market. I was meeting with "Mr. Big Shot" to see if he fit the client profile that the bank was looking for. The longer he pontificated, the more questions he raised in my mind. When he finally finished his sermon of self-importance, he looked sternly at me and said, "So, what do you think about the possibility?" I had taken copious notes in anticipation that I would go back to the bank, share the information with my boss, and be guided by his experience; but Mr. Big Shot said that I needed to make the decision, right then!

In that moment, unsure if my mind was analyzing the scenario correctly, I decided to ignore his intimidation and the fears of losing an important client and draw upon my personal courage. I said, "I don't think this opportunity will be a good fit for us." I immediately got up from my chair, picked up my briefcase, and said, "Thank you for your time."

He was so angry with me that, as I walked toward the office door, he literally got in my face, saying, "This can be a small town. I'll remember you and make you regret this!" He did this all the way to the hallway that housed the elevators.

Wow! Now what would I do? I had no idea if I had screwed up or done the right thing! As I approached my car, I could feel myself shaking as I began to wonder: *Will I be fired? Will I be blacklisted?* I called the bank president, and when he picked up the phone, I said, "You're either going to be pleased with my decision in this prospect meeting, or you're going to fire me today!" He said, "Hold on, I'm in a meeting with the chairman of the board and the vice presidents, and I'm going to put you on speakerphone. What happened?"

Barely able to breathe, I told the story. All five of them immediately cracked up laughing! They recognized that Mr. Big Shot was little more than a self-important bully and not at all the type of client with whom they wanted to associate. The reaction from my boss left me feeling thankful [for taking my calculated risk].

Had she not taken the gamble of adhering to her instinct instead of following what she assumed was the company position, she wouldn't have earned the respect of her boss, proven her judgment, or saved the bank a potential business loan mistake. And even if her boss had said, "You're wrong; we're going to do business with Mr. Big Shot," she could still feel better in her mind about standing up for her position, instead of being afraid to. Even well-calculated risks don't always turn out ideally. As the expression goes, "Sometimes you're the windshield, sometimes you're the bug." You will more often be the windshield if you choose to act in the manner laid out in this book, all of which is intended to give you the justification for acting with courage.

Don't Wallow in Indecision

Every decision is a calculated risk.

Problems are solved by making decisions; problems are avoided by making good decisions. The sooner you make a decision, the sooner you benefit from it. The earlier you make a bad decision, the sooner you can correct it.

The unanimous response from CEOs and C-level executives when I've asked the question, "What's the *most* difficult part of your job?" has been "Responsibility for decisions." And when I've asked them, "What's the *best* part of your job?" the nearly unanimous response has been "Freedom to make decisions."

These CEOs have given me some of their insights on decision making:

- "It's better to have the burden of making them yourself than having to work under decisions others make for you."
- "You will never be sure that you are right, but you have to make them anyway. It's never the slam dunk that you want."
- "If you are absolutely sure you're going to have a successful outcome, make it clear that your team came up with it to share the glory in the decision making. If you are not sure, take it upon yourself and say, 'I recommend this' so you don't share the blame and defeat."
- "If you take a chance and it's rewarding, great. If it's a kick [in the] ass decision, you have to deal with it."
- "You will have many sleepless nights trying to make decisions because you know they can adversely affect people and their families."

- "You want to be the one who makes others' choices. You shouldn't let someone else make yours. A good decision is to tell a subordinate 'You decide' and then support him.
- "Decisions need to be what's best for the whole, not just what's best for you."
- "Get out of bad decisions as soon as you can. Don't hold on."

That being said, people often want decisions made for them. Some crave surrender, and they need authority figures. If you give a sense of concern for their welfare, they want to take your direction. Many prefer to be told what to do because it removes responsibility and risk.

Fear is the biggest hindrance to the risk of decisiveness. Trepidation in making the wrong choice causes you to make none, and then nothing gets accomplished or resolved. Chronic indecision is worse than making bad decisions. And, of course, not making one is a decision in itself.

To decide on a course of action, start by asking these questions:

- What is the outcome I want?
- Why don't I have it?
- What do I need to do to get it?

Gather as many facts as you can till you feel reasonably comfortable. Don't accept suspect facts from others regardless of their role or title. You will never have all the information you want, and there will always be some confusion and frustration in finding out all that you need.

Think of the most wildly successful outcome possible. But don't stop there. Have options. Little is more dangerous than a plan or idea if it's the only one you have. Combine reason with emotion; it's inevitable that both will enter into the equation as you try to be practical. Don't lament and waste energy on things you can't control or wish were different, and don't ignore red flags inside your head.

Mull over the consequences of the decision for now, a month from now, and a year from now too. Still, don't drag your heels (it frustrates people). Roll the dice, and come to a resolution—one that won't land you in the hospital or in prison.

The Marine Corps acronym for their decision-making cycle is OODA: observe, orient, decide, and act—and that's pretty much what I'm suggesting here.

Once you decide, get excited about it. Be specific in your recommendation, and logical in your explanation. State the rationale and why it's the best course of action to pursue. And then be willing to fight for it. Even if you have some doubt, which everyone does, feign certainty because the people you need to influence want decisions made decisively.

In reality, decisions are rarely good or bad. They just are.

Change your mind as you get new information. Don't plead ignorance unless information was deliberately withheld. Never blame problems from your decision on rogue underlings or managers, and don't give public statements that differ from private actions. Sometimes the best decision is to give up on the situation. It's just not worth the fight or the emotional energy because some issues won't get resolved, and continuing to try is where big mistakes happen.

Decisions aren't easy. If they were, they'd already have been made by someone else. Be resolute, but do not be so determined that you refuse to make adjustments. Whatever your solution, frankly, there is a 30 to 40 percent chance that it will work. One study showed that an average of 25 percent of decisions made turn out to be wrong. So when you're wrong, change your mind.

Make Your Share of Mistakes

Even with all your observation, orientation, calculation, evaluation, and rumination, mistakes will occur.

As much as you try to do all things well, you'll make errors; problems won't get resolved, and decisions will turn out badly. One can go from hero to zero pretty quickly—and that's okay, temporarily, because you should be doing things that have a real chance of failure.

Mistakes come with the territory. Everyone makes them. Bill Gates admitted on *60 Minutes* that sometimes his thinking is "sloppy" and he makes mistakes.

CEOs mess up all the time. As some told me:

- "I made some mistakes this morning, and I will make some more later this afternoon."
- "I am the world champion screw-up."
- "I'm all for an employee who makes a successful failure. I've made my share."
- "I purposefully fail in front of my people to set the example that it's permissible."
- "At the executive off-site meeting last month, I gave a $20,000 bonus gift to a team who failed most spectacularly in their sales attempts. I wanted to send the message that I promote people who try big."
- "I have never feared making mistakes because my dad used to say, 'I'll always come visit you in jail' to teach me that I might make bad decisions but that he'd still come and support me."
- "I specifically seek out people to hire and promote who've been banged up a little by mistakes. I want someone who shows resilience and gains wisdom from them. Trust me, that's how I learned."

And that is truly the only reason mistakes are accepted and expected: to learn from.

Make smart mistakes, meaning you tried and failed versus making dumb mistakes where you were too scared and lazy to try. Do things that have some real chance of failure. It's one thing if you've done the right things and lose, but if you didn't try hard enough, if you didn't give enough effort, then that's a different state of affairs. Don't be like the manager who said, "I prefer to live with someone else's mistakes than make my own."

You'll miss, and you'll lose, and you'll fail, but you've just got to get up and start at the grindstone again. It's disappointing, but it's not a shameful loss of face requiring that you retreat to a hermitage. You have to get over it and move on. If you dwell on every loss, you'll do a lot of dwelling. Also, making mistakes really just means you are learning faster. The founder of IBM, Thomas J. Watson, would preach: "The way to succeed is to double your failure rate." How you handle failure either defines or refines you.

Don't panic, freak out, or be scared, but rectify the situation. In business life, it's not what happens. It's how you handle it. You can be devastated and knocked on your backside. Or you can gain valuable lessons from it.

Instead of placing blame, own up. Say, "Oops." Admit it; don't hide or submerge your blunder, just remedy it. Everyone makes mistakes, but not everyone admits them and learns from them. You do, and that's the differentiating factor in your character. The quicker you own up, the more you can get the help you need to put it right and the time to do it.

Do not lay fault elsewhere even if it should be. Be accountable and responsible. Fess up, take care of it, and move on. It isn't a real error until you start to point the finger at others for it. If you make excuses as to why something isn't your fault, you'll lose an opportunity to learn.

Get everyone to decompress. Take a breath. Savor the pain a little. See humor in the strange quirks that led you astray.

You don't get to spend or waste time trying to cop out and get people's understanding and empathy. Don't beat your chest and self-flagellate for show. Ask yourself, and others if fitting, "What went well in the situation? What went poorly? What should I not do again? And what do I need to do now?" Go back to the facts, pull the all-nighter on your own, and reassess. Fix it: find out what you did wrong, and correct or change what you can.

Let failure fuel you. Educate yourself from the experience; that's the best remedy. Failure gives you feedback on what does and does not work, and it provides you an opportunity to try a new direction or approach.

Learn and go on, instead of rehashing, analyzing, scrutinizing, and overly dissecting ad nauseam. Broadly examine the harm done and the consequences from the perspective of all the people involved, even those tangentially. You gain knowledge from trial and error, not trial and rightness.

You will make mistakes. I know, speaking from experience, I've made plenty. I relate to the CEO who said, "I made some mistakes this morning and will make some more later this afternoon."

An off-the-wall idea I had . . . that backfired.

By providing my company's professional development services to a mining company during an industrywide downsizing, I was attempting to help maintain the self-esteem of over 200 employees being caught in massive cutbacks.

I knew the CEO, and I wanted to help him help his people maintain their self-esteem and job skills during the tough times. I also knew that every other consulting firm in the country was reaching out to him too. I wanted to stand out, to be different, to cut through all the clutter.

So I devised a unique approach to send him two dozen depressed-looking flowers with a carefully worded note that said, "Your people are depressed like these flowers. With my help they can be revived." Well, it turned out that his reaction to it was not humorous but rather stunned—more like the horse-head-in-the-bed scene in the first *God-father* movie.

Needless to say, I did not get the assignment, and worse, the CEO put me on his blacklist, big time. He would not answer my calls, my letters, or my apologies. Nor would he accept any communication on my behalf through a third party or from a mutual friend. But I persisted, every six months or so sending an article of interest, note of congratulations, a helpful resource, and more. It took a while for him to be receptive to me again—it was five years to be exact before he finally agreed to let me buy him lunch at his favorite (and very expensive) restaurant.

Conversation was a little cool in the beginning, both of us being professionally courteous in our small talk, community talk, and so on. Finally, the time was right to bring up the elephant in the room—the depressed flowers—and apologize with deepest sincerity.

He let me explain and express regret, and then he said, "At the time, I was extremely mad at you, but I've since come to see your attempt at humor. It was a very difficult time for the company, and the flowers just hit me wrong. But I've been watching you the last five years, and I have to say, I respect you. You are different from most women—well, most people for that matter. You don't ask for permission. You ask for forgiveness. You don't wait until you are invited in. You confidently insert yourself as if you belong. I'm like that too."

We remained professional friends, and later I heard he actually spoke in a fairly complimentary way about me to his peers.

The best way to repair a situation is through stellar work. Be grateful you have the freedom to make mistakes. As long as you get back up, you're winning.

You gain more from one bad decision than all the good decisions you'll ever make. With decisions, when you win, you win; when you don't, you gain knowledge if you attack it well. When you lose, don't lose the lesson from the downbeat experience.

Take consolation in that:

- A lot of mistakes, slipups, and missteps are in the eye of the beholder. You will be harder on yourself than others likely will be.
- Mistakes, like problems, are more interesting and make for better conversation. If you didn't make blunders and gaffes, what would your colleagues have to talk about?
- You might have made a worthless decision, but you aren't a worthless person.
- Few of yours or mine are like Garrett McNamara's, the record-holding surfer I spoke with. He said about the world record wave that he surfed: "If you make a mistake, it could be your last."

- Whatever you did wrong, it will pass. People will forget, at least a little, as they move on to other things. Failure is strictly a temporary condition.
- Only dead people don't make mistakes.

Whatever you do, don't quit trying to do more and to do better in your work. Holding back for fear of a misstep is the biggest mistake you can make. (Still, as mentioned, avoid mistakes that could land you in the hospital or in prison.)

CHAPTER 10

Communicate Well
with a Diverse Group

WHEN IT comes to communication, most people think they do it; few do it well. More is thought to take place than actually does. The most important thing to know is that you cannot communicate too much. Regardless of your job function or title, nothing is gained in a corporate system by avoiding communication.

With good communication skills across a diverse group, you achieve a higher degree of trust, greater motivation and commitment, better coordination between levels, and improvement in operations and efficiency.

Communication is not about being a great orator or going viral on YouTube. It's about knowing what needs to be expressed clearly, how, and to whom. You must ask to find out what must be communicated, and you need to listen to what was said. It's making yourself worth listening to when you speak using relevant stories, examples, or anecdotes. It's about bonding and connecting, not just dispensing data.

With that being said, most communication is usually messy, emotional, irrational, unclear, and disorganized whether in person, over digital media, or by phone.

CEOs say a good communicator is someone who:

- Stays engaged.
- Can carry a conversation.
- Knows what's going on in the world.
- Puts thoughts forward clearly without ambiguity.
- Is able to articulate pretty specifically what he is doing or learning.

- Has the ability to influence without power.
- Is diplomatic.
- Causes connectivity and change instantaneously.
- Expresses herself well, is persuasive, puts things in context, and finds the right phrase to help listeners form an image.
- Thinks about everything he says but doesn't say everything he thinks.

Whether you are trying to share data, formulate thinking, ventilate, establish relationships, guide, assure, inspire, criticize, or persuade, if done without others' interests in mind, you will be ignored or dismissed. Whether for a formal presentation, hallway conversation, or office drop-in, lead with the information that recipients care about most.

Figure Out What the Other Person Wants from the Exchange

In life everyone's top interests are based around oneself. One's self can include immediate family, but it is still primarily oneself. People tune out of the interchange if it doesn't relate to them. To communicate well with people, you must first and foremost relate their interests to yours, finding a common ground and considering their frame of reference.

Most people mistakenly try to commune with their own self-interests first. Adjust your message to how or what your audience needs to hear, not just to what and how you want to say it. You also need to know what you want to get across as you engage and attempt to influence. You can't be like the person who said to me, "I'll know what I want after I hear what I've said." If you don't know for certain what you need, you likely won't get it. Believe me, others won't guess correctly; they won't see between the lines, read your mind, or interpret accurately either.

Observe, consider, study, and ask what the other people care about pertaining to the subject or issue at hand. Again, lead from their interests, not yours. You can find out a lot online about other people's interests: how they interact, their political or social positions, their friends, whom they follow, and who follows them.

You can discover a lot by simply asking straight out what they care about and what they want to have happen in whatever situation you're involved with them. Don't just look between the online lines, trying to read their mind and surmise, guess, or assume the nature of their concerns. Ask questions—if you don't, you won't receive the answers.

One CEO told me a story relating to "knowing your audience" so to speak: "On our twenty-fifth wedding anniversary, I told my wife I'd give her a choice of a 25-carat diamond ring or $250,000, which she could give away to whomever and however she wanted. What do you think she picked?" he asked me.

I said, "Knowing her, I think she chose to give the money away."

"That's right. I make it a practice to know what people want. I was fully prepared to shell out the $2.5 million for the ring, though, if she surprised me and went the other way!"

Be Dialectic: If It Was Good Enough for Plato, It's Good Enough for You

An inquiring mind leads to better communication and avoidance of mutual mystification. Without your incessant clamoring for more information from others, you are fumbling around in the dark. That adds to why most communication is messy, emotional, irrational, unclear, and disorganized. Inquiry takes care of those problems. It makes things clear, rational, and organized when you know and can connect both what you want out of the exchange and what the other people want. You also:

- Gain new information.
- Confirm what you know.
- Make others feel valued and heard.
- Stimulate conversation exchange.
- Avoid acting like a know-it-all.
- Show self-confidence.
- Satisfy your curiosity.
- Get more information to make better decisions and solve problems.

- Can push back without attack.
- Come across as more interesting.
- Create connection and affiliation.
- Buy yourself time.
- Stay on track in conversation.
- Find communal agreement and gain insight as to how to bridge their interests to yours.

Make it your personal rule of thumb to pose at least one question to everyone you engage with during the course of the day. And by "everyone," I mean *everyone*: ask the barista at Starbucks, the teller at the bank, the clerk while picking up dry cleaning, the security guard when you enter your building, the floor receptionist, your assistant, your boss when you run into him in the company cafeteria, your colleague when she calls to get your advice, your customer when he e-mails to complain, your spouse when he texts you to remember your child's soccer game, your child's soccer coach, and your waiter at the pizza restaurant after the game. You should be asking at least one question, preferably more, of anyone you come face-to-face with.

Don't interrogate, but query enough to keep them talking, telling, and explaining. Make sure to volunteer information about yourself or your thoughts as well, so the conversation is not one-sided. If you don't keep it balanced, you look secretive and distrustful.

Knock the Ping-Pong ball back and forth with questions from you, questions from them, questions from you, questions from them. Listen and absorb. Give people an opportunity to grill and argue with you. You don't want sycophants who tell you only the distorted truth.

Choose the tone, facial expression, eye contact, timing, posture, and attitude that will help you get the most collaboration with people. Choose words that draw out what's inside their head:

- "What makes you want to upchuck?" likely gets a better answer than, "What bothers you?"
- "Who are you?" is more abrasive than, "You look familiar. Do I know you?"

- "What part of the meeting was most effective for you?" gets a more detailed answer than "How was the meeting?"
- "What do we need to do to get this part___ done by this time___, and in what format do you want it?" is more directive than, "What do we need to do to get this done?"
- "I know nothing about ___. Would you tell me about it?" will get more cooperation than, "What do you do exactly?"

A good end-of-conversation question is to ask the other person, "Did you say what you needed to say? Did you get what you wanted out of this conversation?"

If you need to persuade, it's especially important to pose questions like the following early and often:

- What do you want to achieve?
- What do you want to have happen?
- What is your goal?
- What is your objective?
- What don't you want to change?
- What do you want to maintain?
- What do you want to avoid?
- What don't you want to have happen?
- When the dust settles, what don't you want to see?
- What would be bad news?
- How would the team react to _____?
- Why do you think _____ worked better here than _____?
- What if we did _____?

Literally after each one of the above, follow the answer to the question with, "Tell me more." Or "Can you give me an example?" Or "Would you paint a picture?" Or "Give that to me again." Or "Put that in layman's terms." People lie, or they are lazy, and you need to get an honest, untold, and clear answer versus just a superficial one. One question seldom does it. Again, don't be tedious or grating. Be interested as you delve deeper into your inquiry. I recommend asking a question three times in three slightly different ways to get "to the truth." One CEO told me, "No, Debra, you need to ask five times!"

Just because you ask and they answer, it doesn't mean the exchange is lucid. Don't assume you know what they mean—most of the time they don't even know. You help them, and you help you, when you ask again and once more and another time. People don't share, tell, or reveal unless you ask lots of times.

And even when you ask, remember that what someone answered can change over time—over a weekend, overnight, and even over lunch. So ask for now, then ask again later. Don't be tiresome, but do be thorough.

Listen Deeply and Long

Silence is part of a good conversation.

A key requirement for communication is meaningful listening. That means when people talk to you or answer your questions, you hear and you remember what they said. That is how you differentiate and rise through the ranks.

It's hard for people to feel engaged with you if they aren't listened to. You give and express respect when you listen. You demonstrate self-confidence in not needing to be the one talking. And you increase your chances of being heard when it's your time to speak.

CEOs tell me:

- "A basic prerequisite to instilling confidence in others is to zip your mouth. Listen to them so you know what they want and they recognize that they've been heard."
- "How did I distinguish myself from other comparable people? I listen better and I have huge retention. In school it was a time saver, and a business meeting isn't a lot different from a college lecture."
- "I have been in millions of drier-than-dirt meetings around the world, but you still have to focus on the people you're with and why you are there. You've got to forget about your boredom. If you try to sneak and read your smartphone under the table,

that's the worst body language you can have in a meeting. Don't pretend to be there. *Be there*."

Don't be absent when you're present. Look into the person's face as he talks to hear the words and see the body language and grasp the emotional subtext.

When you intensely listen to people, they tell you things, things that often others don't know because they didn't pay attention. It's that uncomplicated.

If you go through the effort of observing, studying, and asking questions but aren't mentally and emotionally present, it's a waste of your time and theirs. If your mind is someplace else, it shows in your body, eyes, and face.

Ignore your phone, and don't doodle, look at your mobile device, stare out into space, glance toward others when they come into your field of vision, get up and get coffee, fidget, or squirm. Don't divide your attention with other people or goings on.

Don't speak when other people are. Don't finish their sentences for them or talk over the end of theirs. If you accidentally do, stop, apologize, and don't do it again, or the apology is viewed as a lie. Take notes. Ask a question to clarify or confirm what you're hearing. Intersperse your listening with an occasional, "Ahhh, I get it." Or "I see." Or "Now I understand." Or "Thanks for the clarification."

Stop the voice inside your head. Don't be playing your own Ping-Pong game of thoughts.

Don't think about what you are intending to say because you can't listen if you're just planning to speak the whole time. Resist the urge to interrupt, reply, and blurt out responses. Exercise restraint; bite your tongue. Concentrate on understanding the person, not on framing your reply. Resist the urge to defend yourself, explain yourself, or offer quick fixes. The only internal dialogue should be open-minded inquiry:

- What don't I know about the situation?
- What's really going on here?
- What does the other person know or believe that makes her see the world differently from the way I see it?

Confirm what you heard. Step back, and take in what others know and say so you can fuse it with your own thinking. Then go and do something with what you heard.

Cathi Hight, president of the Hight Performance Group, says, "People screen out or change the intended purpose of what they hear in over 70 percent of all communication." Refrain from that tendency if for no other reason than that you don't want it done to you. Set the pattern.

The less you say, the more it appears that you are listening. I asked a CEO one time, "Why do bosses nod and not say anything?" He answered, "If we say something, you aren't talking, and if we leave a long silence, you'll fill it in and incriminate yourself."

Speak up, but do so only after you slow down and think. Although it's always a good thing to shut up, remain silent, and listen long and hard, you are there for one reason, and that is to contribute. If you remain hushed for too long, no one will listen to you. Think, then speak in a manner that gets heard and received in the best way possible.

Choose Your Words with Care

Good communication is when you haven't said things that you wish you'd left unsaid. You choose your spoken and written words with care to make sense and interest the listener or reader. And you avoid "verbal vomit" as one CEO explained, "spewing without thought."

You get positive attention from higher-ups when in a straightforward manner you clearly sum up "the guts of your opinion" followed with offering to elaborate if needed.

You refrain from:

- Using jargon, buzzwords, and clichés.
- Dense, dull, impersonal, abstract, and deliberately obfuscatory words.
- Repeating the same words (because brains ignore overused words).
- Chattering away and being wordy and tedious.

You persist in your efforts to:

- Think and rethink the words you talk or type.
- Use colorful, fresh, sharp, and hard-sounding words versus mushy ones.
- Rehearse in your head the words before they cross your lips, even saying them out loud to yourself to hear how they sound.
- Be unconvoluted.
- Be brief, clear, precise, and to the point. (For example, try to boil 120 words of what you plan to say down to 50, then down to 25 words, then 6, and finally 1.)

CURSING IS AN OPTION

I once wrote an op-ed piece suggesting that the occasional, selective, and judicious use of profanity is one more communication tool in your belt because it shows passion, conviction, and confidence, it initiates a shared emotional response, and it fosters bonding.

I had surveyed over 100 CEOs and C-suite execs, and among the respondents, 80 percent of men admitted using profanity, and 13 percent of women did so.

The *Wall Street Journal* was quick to point out, "This advice isn't likely to appear in books on business." Yet here it is. I've seen people successfully use expletives for shock and humor and to diffuse tension.

One CEO, who was also a licensed psychologist, told me that he instructs his managers to ask job candidates if they would object to profanity in the office. A "yes" answer may indicate a judgmental "holier than thou attitude," which in his opinion could hurt teamwork.

If you choose to use it, here are some ground rules:

- Swear with purpose at an appropriate time and in a calm tone of voice.
- Never mumble or mutter it under your breath.
- Always aim it at projects, issues, or situations, *never* at people.

Most important, do not be judgmental when others use it around you. An objection is definitely an "I'm okay, you're *not* okay" reaction that is counter to what I'll write about in Chapter 12 on giving acceptance.

Personally speaking, I'd rather people curse in front of me than text while I'm speaking to them.

Tell Tales

Anything you want to get across is better explained with well-told narratives, examples, analogies, or anecdotes. Make them short, relevant, and with a takeaway message. People forget lists, bullet points, even facts, but they remember well-told stories, which will:

- Help people with different frames of reference relate and understand each other.
- Help you share knowledge in an interesting and memorable way.
- Help people develop affinity.
- Give an example of how things play out because they make situations familiar and comfortable to relate to.
- Convey complex information in a comprehensible way.
- Simplify a complicated situation.
- Enable you to tell things people need to know about you without your bragging or tooting your horn.
- Make your whole brain work and become more active, both in the telling and the listening.

When you tell a tale, you want to get these kinds of responses: "Wow, I would have never thought that would happen." "Okay, I get it." "Geesh, I'm glad that didn't happen to me." "Hmmm, never thought about it that way." "That's so right." "Now I understand." Ideally, it's a good story they will remember for the rest of their life.

Keep it simple: cause and effect. Think in terms of the format for a joke: the setup, the story, and the punch line:

- *Set the scene.* That way, you start off from a point of mutual understanding with whomever you're communicating with.
- *Tell what happened then.* Describe what was done and the action you took. Relay the difficulty that was overcome or the hurdle, obstacle, strife, adversity, or setback that was conquered.
- *Tell what resulted.* To wrap up your story, briefly explain the outcome, resolution, or transformation that emerged. A happy, positive, or successful ending works, but a negative one causes a visceral response.

As you plan the narrative, sharpen the details and add honest color and momentum. One of my favorite lines is from an old rocker who talked about where the lyrics for his song came from: "riding shotgun in a Corvette with a drug dealer on the way to a poker game and then the cops came." Be honest and logical; don't stretch or exaggerate. Incorporate humor, nostalgia, even disgust. They make for good stories.

Illustrate your point using sight, sound, smell, and touch. Use colorful words. Personalize with "I" or "We." Keep editing until it's tight.

Collect, develop, and hone your stories. Keep them complete but also short. Talk in as many half-minutes as you can get, but never talk more than a half-minute without giving others the opportunity to contribute to the conversation.

If you can add a humorous angle, end, or spin to your story, it will be even better. People relax, and they learn better when entertained. With judicious gentle humor, you illustrate your point better, take blows, diffuse tense situations, poke fun at yourself to keep your ego from being tied up in it, show your good nature, demonstrate courage and self-confidence, differentiate yourself, improve communication, and assert your adequacy and equality.

Now, it can also get you in trouble if you don't weigh your words, consider your audience, and have the right tone and mindset. So practice, rehearse, and try your story out privately before going public.

Even with your best attempt to communicate well with a diverse group, there will be some people who don't "get it" or "get you." That's life. Remember that you too don't always "get" others. The differentiator is that you don't let that get you down. You keep on truckin'. (Oh, and when they don't laugh, you can say with a smile on your face, "Hmmm, I guess that was a thinking man's joke.")

Touch to Bond and Connect

Touch, like profanity is a delicate communication tool—but it is one that can positively differentiate you. If you think about it, a lot that you do in life is touch related. Figuratively, you "get in touch," "stay in touch," "will be in touch," and "get back in touch." I'm just recommending that you do it literally also.

Years ago, at a *Fortune* magazine conference, I sat beside a television production CEO. When he spoke to me, he put both hands on my shoulders to draw me in closer. I observed he did the same to everyone else—men and women. I asked about his technique, and he said it was to ensure that what he said got heard. He could have accomplished the same thing by talking louder, but his making that actual physical contact was better.

The benefits of appropriate touch far outweigh the drawbacks. When you touch, you connect, bond, develop an affinity, build a bridge, display self-confidence, and set yourself apart.

Many times words are not sufficient. You must reach out and touch someone. If a picture paints a thousand words, appropriate physical contact conveys 10 times that. Touch someone when you want to congratulate, compliment, calm, sympathize, affect, influence, inspire, get attention, and make a point. Touch can be done in a job interview, a board meeting, a job termination meeting, a sales call, or a negotiation. Anytime you want your words and meaning to have more weight, differentiate yourself with the legitimate communication tool of touch.

In a job interview, a two-handed handshake might be better than a one-handed handshake for conveying extra comfortableness with the person you're meeting. In a board meeting, putting one hand on another person's shoulder as you get close to discuss something signifies more importance. In a job termination situation, you've already been fired, so surprise the person with a hug. (I guarantee she will never forget it.) In a sales call, the two-handed handshake or hand on the shoulder as you make a point conveys your conviction and enthusiasm. And if a contract has been signed, your second hand on the person's elbow is even better. In a negotiation, as you stand up to get a bottle of water for yourself, you could touch your opponent's forearm as you offer, "Could I get a bottle for you too?" which could diffuse some innate animosity. Any one of those microgestures can change the tone of a meeting. None of those gestures imply an inappropriate touch—that is, a lascivious, fawning, or smarmy touch. All of them involve laying your hands on someone's hand, shoulder, or forearm only.

And again, you may be asking, "Why?" It's to set you apart and differentiate you in a positive, memorable, impressive, confident way. One of my favorite CEOs told me his approach. (But first, I need to add, he's 6 feet 4 inches, 270 pounds—rather imposing.) He said: "Every time I meet new people, I give them a bear hug. They either relax and enjoy it or go catatonic, but they never forget it."

You can't imagine a sporting game where celebratory, congratulatory, supportive touch isn't allowed. Why should the game of business be any different?

Yes, it can be uncomfortable, misinterpreted, and even get you sued—*if* executed inappropriately and with the wrong attitude. So do it well with the attitude to connect, build a bridge, and bond.

Be consistent. Everyone gets the same thing—men, women, bosses, subordinates, peers, competitors. Yes, everyone up and down the ladder gets the same. Don't touch only the people you know and like; do the same with people you don't know yet or don't like. You can get in trouble if you do it selectively.

I've been told this: "The reason guys get in trouble is that they touch the young, pretty ones they are attracted to. They need to be consistent and touch the old, ugly, scary ones too."

Choose an appropriate part of the other person's body, above the waist on a shoulder or forearm. Firmly lay your hand on, hold a split second, and calmly retreat from the touch. Slow and purposeful versus fast and jerky takes courage, shows confidence, and gives meaning to the recipient.

You don't need to have a cuddle party or hug fest. You don't want to need a sign like the ones in the prison visiting rooms: "No hugging. No kissing. No handshakes."

If you sense a negative response, privately but quickly inquire if you have offended. If the answer is "yes," apologize and ask what he wants you to do to set it right. If the answer is "No, I was just surprised," say, "Good, because I sincerely meant. . . ."

Avoid self-touch. Pinching or wiping your nose, touching the corners of your mouth, stroking your check, rubbing your eyes—all put germaphobics on edge. Avoid these gestures at all costs.

Communication is a big subject to address in one chapter; the part of the subject that I'm trying to get across is how to make it a huge differentiator for you. If by making pointed inquiries, you find out what others' interests, goals, objectives, and desires are first, you'll be miles ahead of others who go into situations with their own purpose first and foremost. And even when you think you know what other people are thinking and feeling, you need to keep gently probing, not prodding, further. This will allow you to hear deeper meanings and will enable you to connect your purpose with those of other people. Another differentiator is that you will use any tool possible to ensure an effective exchange: stories, touches, even expletives. Because the world is diverse, you have to have diverse ways to make the magic happen.

CHAPTER 11

Don't Be a Sycophant

I F YOU strongly disagree with an approach, a task, an injustice, or anything that pertains to achieving the company's or your own mission, tell your boss how you feel directly. If you have information that differs from the boss's position or point of view that will genuinely move the company forward, not just move you forward, you have to talk to her. You can still be loyal, support your boss, be respectful, and try to make her life easier, but in an honest, confident manner, you have to express your beliefs.

Speak up when you think he is on target or not. Bosses need to hear it when you think they are right, just as they need to hear it when you think they are wrong. A confident person holds to her own ideas, which may not be the boss's.

Don't be a sycophant. Push back. As one CEO told me, "A reverberation of your own thoughts is okay for a little while, but you soon get tired of it."

To push back does not mean to argue with no merit or to be a troublemaker or rabble-rouser for no reason. It means to pleasantly but assertively question. And it means to get to an understanding of what she is saying, and then explain how and why you see it differently.

You needn't do it in a throw-down, go-toe-to-toe, whine-kick-and-scream, verbal-fisticuffs, threatening, or open-conflict way. As one CEO put it, "Just speak up as if you've never been shushed. Have a meaningful discussion. Be reasonable with a smile."

In general, I'd refrain from pushing back in the manner of one CEO who relayed a story from early in his engineering career. He had a toxic manager that everyone was afraid to confront. The young engineer had

had enough of the back stabbing. He went into his manager's office one day, climbed up on the chair facing the desk and then onto the desk, stared down at the colleague and said, "My impulse is to kick the sh** out of you if you don't turn your behavior around." The CEO told me, "Needless to say, he treated me differently from then on, and he stopped his undermining of my work."

I'd recommend an approach more like that of Richard Toeppe, vice president of manufacturing for Fenner-Dunlop, who told me about a boss of his who micromanaged Richard's subordinates inappropriately and in front of people he shouldn't have. This action undermined Richard, sent mixed messages to his people about who was in charge, and caused the subordinates to be reticent to speak up. So Richard called him up on the phone, and in a pleasantly assertive, pass-the-salt tone of voice, he asked if the boss's expectations had been met at the last meeting, which had included Richard's team. "They were," the boss said. Then Richard said:

> You see, I don't think your goal was achieved, but rather just the opposite. By your going around me to direct my team in the meeting, you were undermining my authority. I have responsibility for the operations, but responsibility without accountability destroys leadership. Your action creates confusion in my own directions and role. It appears to the team that you lack trust in my ability. Now if you have issues with my ability, we need to address this now before we go any further.

Richard went on to tell me that when he finished explaining the issue to his boss, the boss said he was sorry and that he had complete confidence in Richard's abilities. "He said that micromanaging was one of his flaws. However, he was surprised I would address it because no one had ever called him out on it in a professional way before. He told me to make sure I help him in future when he gets in a micro mode. Since the conversation, we have been working together very well."

I know, it takes confidence and courage to speak up, but it's better to be uncomfortable and strong than still. The short time it takes to correct poor behavior is better than the long time you suffer putting up with it.

Another reasonable approach came from two different CEOs who recalled a time earlier in their careers when they had to talk tough love to the boss. One said, "From the start of my career, after discussing a problem, I'd tell my boss, 'If you don't have a better idea than mine, I'm taking mine.'" And the other CEO told me the line that he used when necessary was, "I'd agree with you, but then we'd both be wrong."

The whole package: your attitude, comportment, and track record have to be in place to carry off those kind of statements. You've got to produce good work to do this; it's not for the unproven newbie, new hire, or even newly promoted.

A singular situation involved a couple of VPs who were being considered for a division presidency. The CEO and the VPs were in a strategy meeting focusing on the CEO's recommendations. Both VPs were strong performers who had exceeded company expectations, but one VP on occasion would vigorously speak up in private with the CEO against his suggestions. She always finished her argument with, "That being said, I am a team player. I will go along with your decision. . . . [sometimes adding a little humor with] . . . You're the man!" She clearly spoke her mind about the issue she disagreed with and made her position clear, but she also supported her boss as long as what he wanted to do was legal, moral, and ethical.

The other VP in this particular meeting disagreed with the CEOs position, too, but she chose not to confront him. Instead, she silently seethed under her breath and soon after complained to her subordinates. Two weeks later, the announcement was made for the new division president, and it was the one who had argued with her boss. The CEO told me, "If I wanted someone to just go along with me, I wouldn't be getting what I need. I try to talk them out of agreeing with me. It's poison to me when people acquiesce. I will fire a person for it."

No one, including your boss, should hinder you from doing your job, and if agreeing with the supervisor because of the title hinders you, you owe it to yourself to speak up. CEOs tell me:

- "I want people to pick a fight with me, . . . but not ad nauseum. . . . Still they can disagree pretty vigorously."
- "Argue with me? Absolutely. I try to encourage it. I'm a very direct person, and I don't like people sitting back quietly. I'd always rather hear what is on people's mind. No good comes from quiet disagreement. The most valuable people on my team are willing to disagree with me."
- "I want a culture of bluntness: they can be that way with me, and I can be that way with them."
- "If you have the courage to say 'no' versus 'yes,' it gets you promoted."
- "If I give my opinion and all four people in the room say it's a good thought, I don't need those four people. I want them to give me *their* ideas, not mine. It's a dangerous situation if I hear the same thing without dispute from my people."
- "I hate 'yes' people. I love rabble-rousers. I have one now, and people ask, 'Why don't you fire him?' I say, 'I call him to tell me what's not right.'"
- "I have an employee whom all the executives label a miscreant. We battle on everything. One of my officers asked, 'Why do you put up with him?' I said, 'He's the only one who tells me I'm wrong, and sometimes he's right.'"

One EVP I spoke with had been in the Israeli army as a youth, and she told me about the culture of irreverence that is encouraged in the army: "If the most junior person doesn't challenge you, you create blind spots."

Don't talk trash to colleagues or subordinates behind a boss's back. Talk to the boss directly. As one manager put it, "People are more verbal over a beer in a pub than they are up-front and outspoken over glasses of bottled water in a boardroom." If you're going to state disagreement, say it privately but directly to the person you disagree with.

Instead of just being good at following the CEO's ideas and directions, have your own that you contribute. Give valid reasons for your recommendations. Have knowledge and information that out-details and out-facts them. Clearly put your evaluation, opinion, and options out there with candor, directness, objectivity, and respect.

Use an even tone of voice, square your shoulders, look 'em in the eye, and give a comfortable smile.

Negative response need not be given in a negative way: "You were right on target when you said . . . , and to follow your lead, I did some research on my own that you'll want to see as we define and refine our position," will be better received than, "You're wrong. I don't know how you came up with that, but I found out the truth, and it's totally different from what you said. The only way it can go is. . . . It's stupid any other way."

The best way to choose your words when you need to push back is to clearly know what you need to say and then say it to the other person the way you would like it said to you. It's a big differentiator for you to pause, consider if you were in that person's Cole Haans how you would like to be talked to, and then weigh your words and harness your tone of voice, facial expression, and comportment.

Avoid any emotional lashing out, fist pounding, or shouting. And of course, do not insinuate, insult, or peck away at a person's character or morals (which is discussed in the next chapter) because doing so is being critical and judgmental, not disagreeing with valid reasoning.

Don't fold when the person challenges you. Instead of telling your boss what he wants to hear, stick with the facts as you see them.

With all that being said, until you are the boss, the CEO, or the top dog, at the end of the day, you do have to go along with the boss's verdict. If you've clearly and responsibly made your position known, you have to go with the boss's plan until you become the boss. The boss's decisions may be right, not your recommendations, despite your veracity in thinking otherwise. One reason is that the boss is likely to have more and different data than you are privy to because of her position.

Keep this in mind: the higher up, the more information your manager has and therefore the broader his perspective. Just as you are privy to more facts and stats than your people are, your boss is given more than you. Yes, your continuous curiosity on a wide range of subjects helps you get more information on your own, but still, bosses win battles because they have access to more inside insight and information.

I'm clearly for you setting yourself apart by wisely, judiciously, and effectively arguing your position and point of view when you have valid reasons and knowledge. But even when you do it in an exemplary fashion, make sure you are right most of the time. If you occasionally or repeatedly fight for your position and it turns out to be going in the wrong direction, you're likely fighting just to fight, not to make the work situation better.

Fight for what you absolutely, passionately believe up until the minute someone proves you wrong.

DON'T OVERDO IT

Don't battle with the boss on e-v-e-r-y-t-h-i-n-g. Be selective as to what really matters in achieving the group's goals. Anything illegal or immoral or that inhibits you from doing your job and achieving the company mission is especially fair game to push back on.

But don't get carried away with every bothersome thing. Difficult situations happen all the time to all levels of workers so don't make every issue, despite your disagreement, an argument. Pick the most egregious issue to tackle. Don't start a war with your supervisors or colleagues every single time that they do any of the following:

- Ask for your input when they have already made a decision
- Take credit for something they didn't do
- Insert themselves into your territory without explanation
- Micromanage
- Totally disregard the feelings and needs of customers and employees
- Change a procedure but don't tell you it has been changed
- Blame mistakes on employees

- Tell you something in confidence and say not to repeat it, then tell others the same, as if looking for spies
- Hire you for your ability, but then not want your input or involvement in your area of expertise in the process or procedures
- Tell you something you know to be untrue, but due to the "level of command," you have to let it pass for truth
- End every request with "Do you think you can do that?" as if there's some doubt
- Train you in a nonlinear fashion so you get only some of the pieces of the puzzle
- Continually praise one or two people rather than acknowledging the efforts of everyone on the team
- Tell you how to handle something on the first day and then change their mind on the next day
- Get in the way of getting the job done
- Don't talk to you for four months and then give you a bad evaluation
- Ignore you
- Don't reply to multiple requests, e-mails, and phone messages for days or sometimes weeks

Sycophants breed sycophants. The employee a good boss is most afraid of is a "suck-up." Managers don't simply want "yes" people to lazily agree with all of their decisions. They will also believe that you expect your subordinates to do the same to you.

As one CEO put it, "There are people who kiss your backside, then expect theirs to be kissed, which exacerbates the trouble. Sometimes the worst offender is the CEO to his own board of directors." Another joked, "It would have screwed up my career if I couldn't be one"—he was kiddingly saying (with some truth to it, I'm sure) that he had gotten where he was by being a sycophant.

The problem is that not all bosses dislike sycophants. Some really like them. Think about it: who doesn't love someone who says everything we do is right, brilliant, and perfect in our thinking, in our decisions, and in our problem solving? Of course, it's natural to like affirmation for all we do. Insecure people really like it because it feeds their ego.

Because "yes" people and toadies butter up the boss's ego, they usually get a lot of time and attention from the boss. It's human nature to want the flattery that comes with agreement over contradiction.

And bluntly, it's easier to run an organization because nothing stops the boss from getting what she wants. I heard a not-so-good executive say this: "I don't care what you believe as long as you don't tell me."

Your boss tests you in some areas. It's reasonable for you to test him too. As one told me, "A very confident person will try to intimidate me to see if I can handle it and to see if he wants to work with me."

"How do they do it effectively?" I asked.

"They throw zingers at me with good humor. Sort of an, 'I'm okay, you're okay.' That's fine. The approach I don't like is an, 'I'm okay, you're *not* okay' attitude with me or anyone else," he explained.

Your objective is to make your boss successful, but that does not mean that you unjustifiably flatter her, agree with her, be a "yes" person, a toady, or a kiss-up, or just go along with her because of her role. Don't defer.

If you have a boss whose toxic environment encourages sycophants and it is undeniably and unquestionably so, get away from that person if possible.

In actuality, people work for not-so-good supervisors all the time, all over the world. So keep these points in mind: One, don't be that type of person yourself. Two, don't reward that type of behavior if possible. And three, still learn to work with that type of person because you'll find people like him everywhere.

CHAPTER 12

Cause Others to Do Well

Everything I've written in this book leads to this concept: if you aren't a quality individual, you can't positively affect others. And if you *are* such a person—that is, trusted, comfortable in your own skin, easy to get along with, able to engage others, and doing a stellar job—it all amounts to nothing unless you can help others in those endeavors as well.

People assisting other people in achieving their day-in-day-out grind, not just their end goals, happens less than you would think—that's why it's a big differentiator for you if you do it. Putting it candidly, you need to cause people around you to be successful because if they fail, you fail—and you, of course, don't want that.

It's only at the *entry* level where you're assessed by what you alone produce. At every other level, you are evaluated on how you affect people around you. Being an indispensable solo performer isn't enough. You have to help make others up and down the ladder be indispensable too. When you cause people around you to be accomplished and to feel valued, strong, and talented, you're the one who shines.

You get noticed and "pulled up from above" as well as "pushed from below" because of what you trigger others to attain.

You and your work value are evaluated in two ways:

- First, *your track record* of productivity and results as compared to that of your peers in achieving your mission
- Second, your effect on *other people's track records* of productivity and results in achieving their mission

CEOs tell me:

- "To truly elevate your game—to evolve—something inside of you has to shift to your understanding that you have significance in this life only if it's not about you."
- "The type of track record I look for is the kind of impact you have, the kind of relationships you leave in the wake."
- "There is no single domino standing alone out there. If one goes, we all go."
- "I lose trust in people who put their own agenda before the group agenda."
- "If the person to the right and the person to the left of you doesn't do well, your work is wasted."

Look out for people. It makes it easier to get things done when they know you care about them and their development. If you keep their interests at heart, they'll take care of you. If people don't believe you'll look out for their interests, they won't look out for yours.

Give Acceptance

The first order of business in aiding others to achieve their mission is to help them maintain self-esteem. Assume high motives and no evil intentions on their part; give acceptance to individuals. Never hire or promote people, however, whose character, motives, and abilities you doubt. But when you do hire someone, grant acceptance as you yourself expect acceptance (as discussed in Chapter 1).

One CEO explained his approach of giving acceptance: "One-third of my employees I'd walk on water for, one-third are so-so, and one-third I would do without if I could do without. My job is to make sure no one knows which group they are in." The idea is similar to family members you are forced to put up with.

When you start interacting with people, you haven't a clue as to their character, morals, motives, abilities, or ambitions. Your obligation is to treat people as if they are broadly adequate and fully capable.

Wholehearted, nonjudgmental approval is the most critical element to dealing with others and the greatest contribution you can give. Show it in your face, choice of words, your listening, and comportment. Anything else is practicing moral superiority, and you'll give off the notion, "I'm okay, but you *aren't* okay."

Give acceptance regardless of their idiosyncrasies, human frailties, secrets, selfishness, cross-purposes, or what their mom and dad taught them. See fewer of their faults, tune out a lot of the negative or judgmental rumblings going on inside your head, and check your own biases or prejudices at the door. Have good forget-ability about their transgressions (alleged or otherwise), and give them the benefit of the doubt. (By the way, this works in a marriage and in your relationships with your extended family, neighbors, and civic contacts too.)

The difference between the amateur and the pro is that the amateur judges people against his own standards and experiences; he expects people to react to stimulus in the same way that he does. A pro does not do that. Nor does she assign her character and morals, motivations, or ambitions to others. A pro tries to find out about and understand other people's backgrounds and frames of reference. Anyone can work well with people she relates to. A pro works well with someone he doesn't relate to. Go slow in judging people.

The first and most important reason for accepting a person's character and motives is that doing so enables you to talk to him about his behavior without being critical. I overheard an executive who practices this type of I'm-okay-you're-okay attitude say: "No offense given [when giving constructive feedback]." His subordinate replied: "None taken"—because of the supervisor's consistent attitude, comportment, and intent. If you don't give acceptance, even simple differences can turn into contradictions, heat, resentment, contentiousness, and conflict.

Often you need to be blunt in the directions you give to people. You can do that successfully only if they don't feel judged or criticized.

The second reason to give acceptance is this: Who are you (or I) to judge anyway? If you had the exact same upbringing, parenting, and experiences the person you are critical of had, you (and I) would be just like her.

If you are disparaging of a person's character or motive, he will not help, support, trust, or respect you, nor push you up from below.

And third, when you accept others, you give them permission to push back, speak up, speak out, and not be a sycophant to you because they know you won't judge, criticize, or punish them for it. This is an extremely significant trait of an exemplary leader: to have people's trust. A positive long-term relationship starts with you and the way you view and treat people. Your title, position, and power means nothing. The only thing that matters is your consistent, genuine, honest, nonjudgmental attitude toward them.

Now on the flip side, if you don't have a boss who has read this book and doesn't practice what I preach, don't skip out on him. If he exudes unproductive behavior with you, it's likely that he does it with others too. Instead of trying to get out from under a boss or around a colleague that you don't initially like, accept her character and motives, and be willing to work with her, at least for now. Later you can change and get away from her, but learn what you can before you exit. You can acquire as much knowledge about appropriate and inappropriate behavior from a bad boss as you can from a good boss.

Try to get to know, like, and respect the person. It is a huge differentiator if you are the one person a difficult individual gets along with or can work with. You will never like everyone you team up with or report to, just as not everyone will like you. But leaders emerge from the masses when they can rise above prejudgment. As one CEO put it: "Put up with people who don't think and act like you. Put up with people you don't enjoy. Put up with less-than-ideal situations. Put up with crap you don't deserve." You might be the person who can bring out the best of the best in them. Any average person can deal with easygoing people. Dealing with difficult people tests your strength of character. When you do it well, you separate yourself from the rest, and you might be able to turn a relationship around into a prolific one that others have failed in. Be the kind of coworker to others that you'd like to have yourself.

Acting in such a manner is not so that you will be liked by others; your being liked is irrelevant. It is so that when you talk to people about what you need from them, they will actually listen, thus increasing your chance of getting what you need to complete a task or job.

To give acceptance and help maintain the self-esteem of others is not an altruistic act. People will soon forget what you've accomplished, but they will long remember how you made them feel about themselves.

If I asked you to name the last five CEOs at the top of the Fortune 50 list or the last few *Time* magazine "person of the year" winners or the last five Nobel or Pulitzer Prize winners, you might not come up with a very complete or accurate response. But if I asked you to name the five people who helped you through a difficult time, who taught you something worthwhile, or made you feel appreciated, you'd come up with those names without a problem. The people who make a difference in your life aren't the ones with the most applause, achievements, awards, credentials, or money. They're the ones who respect you and encourage your self-respect.

Now if a person proves overwhelmingly, unequivocally, undeniably, irrefutably, unquestionably, and repeatedly that he lies, steals, or cheats or engages in illegal or unethical behavior, you have to act on it right away. Only at this point of no return can you be suspicous of his motives or character. If this person is your boss, quit. If she is a subordinate, fire her. If he is a colleague, request a transfer. Do not do it gradually. Flip the toggle switch, tell her, and without delay remove yourself from dealings with her.

The biggest waste of time is the period that falls between when you know someone lies or steals and the time it takes you to separate yourself from the relationship. Note: If you fire someone for lying, he must see it as such. It can't just be your opinion (because a lie is in the eye of the beholder, remember?). Remember, in terms of honesty, one person's view about a situation can be as true to oneself as another's view can be true to that person. So if you're firing someone for lack of honesty, she has to see the dishonesty as you see it, or she will feel you are the one in the wrong.

Also, you don't give approval forever if a person is a poor doer and needs to change behavior. You watch, observe, talk to, get to know, and discuss so as to gather information. Then make up your mind whether you need to flip the switch on that person.

Even at that point, don't scold, be snarky, or chastise. Don't attempt to get back at him and teach him a lesson. Don't give a disgusted face, freeze him out, get outraged, or take a condescending attitude.

Long before you flip that toggle switch, make sure you've done your job in communicating your expectations: what you want and what you don't want in the person's behavior as it affects your doing your own job. If you assume she knows your goals and standards, you will be wrong. If you assume he should think and act as you do, you will be doubly wrong.

Set Expectations, and Then Limit Behavior You Don't Want

Lots of people get a job done but don't get it done right. Aside from entry-level positions, many times, you get things done, complete tasks, and finish projects through other people. You as an individual can only do so much. So if you get someone to do well an extra 10 percent of what you need and then get 10 people doing that extra 10 percent in a stellar fashion, you're going to get a lot of work completed. These colleagues or subordinates become an effective extension of yourself. And in every practice you put into place, you set a solid precedent and good example for them to follow with their people.

If you set the standard of behavior you expect and then you yourself live up to it, your people will more likely do the same for their people. Good leadership behavior filters down (but bad does too). "I want this, not this. Got it? Good. Now go and do it." That is far better than "You should have known I want this, not this. I thought I could count on you. I guess I have to spell things out, and even then I'm not sure if you can follow it. Geesh."

Whether dealing with subordinates, vendors, colleagues, clients, customers, even bosses (to the degree possible), set expectations and boundaries in advance. Be consistent in these expectations with everyone. Make them a major talking point. Don't just mention them during idle conversation. Be outspoken and clear as to what you want and what you don't want from people who report to you and whom you work with. Honestly, it's less doable upward (that is, with your manager or your boss), but at least you can work with your team in that manner.

Tell people why you're doing what you're doing. Be clear about why you have these expectations and why you think they are reasonable and positive for the team. Let them know as much as you can. In the absence of clear direction, people will take their own. But don't overcomplicate things.

If you're in a position to delegate, set expectations and give people meaningful stretch assignments: a challenge with definite responsibilities. Then hold them accountable. Guide them toward what you want, but encourage them to come up with ideas so that they can be the owners of them. Do not say, "I have a great idea, and here's how I want you to carry it out." Instead, even if you had the idea already, say, "Let's kick something around. I need a fresh idea."

Then say, "You tell me what you need from me to do your job" and "Go take your best shot at it, and tell me if that doesn't work." Again after stating your clear expectations, let subordinates run with their idea and come back with the results. Don't hold their hand through the process. Cease overcontrolling, micromanaging, or nitpicking everything your people say and do. If you don't, your overbearing behavior will drive people crazy and cause them to feel that you think they can't do the job, which will also ding their self-esteem.

Just for an example: let subordinates conduct meetings and conversations with other key people without your being present. You instill confidence in others when you allow them to take a risk, come up with answers, and gain courage. Don't interrupt or correct them in public, but do praise them publicly. Don't micromanage. Instead, answer their questions, and then say, "Go for it. It's your baby." Allow them to make mistakes as long as they learn from them. Let them represent you to higher-ups. Give them more of a challenge than they themselves think they can handle. Don't compete with them, show them up, or point out where they were wrong. Instead, give them explanations about better solutions, and act like they came up with them. Attribute any successes to them, any failures to yourself.

Be the initiator of upward communication to your manager, downward to your subordinates, and back to you. Information must constantly flow between you and the people you are working with: boss, team, and colleagues. Be accessible. People need to know they have an entrée to you on any matter and that it's okay to ask for help, report a problem, or admit mistakes.

Be there to give advice whenever asked. Your people don't need to be told everything, but they do need to be able to ask anything. Be visible, reachable, and connected to all levels of the organization; mingle in the company cafeteria, walk the hallways, shake hands, touch, smile, and ask questions.

You should have an "I'm always willing to talk" policy, though not necessarily an open-door policy. When people pop in with the request "I just need five minutes of your time," you have some options. If you think you can resolve the issue right then, you can say, "Okay, five minutes, but then I'm getting back to what I'm working on," and at five minutes, stand up and say, "Now give it your best shot."

If you do stellar work as laid out in this book, you will be very busy. But since you are so stellar, lots of people will want to talk to you. They have many reasons: to get in your good graces, to get your assurances that they are on the right track, to get your opinions and learn from you, to pass on information, to kick around ideas, and to ventilate. Not all of that helps you with what you are working on, and some of it will destroy your own productivity if you tolerate everyone and anyone knocking on your door for "five minutes."

A reasonable response is "Let's make an appointment time to talk. Here are two times I'm available." Or if you have an assistant, you can always say, "Call my assistant, and she'll set that up." Don't deal with problems on your feet and let people take your time unless it is of your choosing. You have to stay in control of your time to get done what you need to. Always be willing to schedule time to listen, to ask, to respond, to think, and to talk things through. Another option is to have a set time such that, for example, every Friday afternoon your door is open, and during that time anyone can walk in and discuss something.

Don't be rigid like having a "guard dog at the gate," and don't avoid, ignore, or leave people hanging. But do be available at a time and place of your choosing.

Manage your time; that's your coin. Subordinates and colleagues can't manipulate your time. You regulate the time you give them. Now, generally speaking, I'd make time for my boss's request for "five minutes," but even then, hold him to it. If you're doing your job well, you're really busy. Well, he should be too, so get in and get out with as clear communication as possible, as discussed in Chapter 10. Note also that it's extremely important to spend those five minutes on what he wants to discuss. There are only as many minutes in the day as you make good use of. People who differentiate themselves give more of those minutes to areas with the most impact.

Whichever approach you use, make reasonably quick decisions. This will guard against stifling the individual efforts of the people you work with. Your example will stimulate achievement and let them exercise creativity and employ their talents. As one manager put it, "Squeeze all the productivity out of people you can."

Remove red tape and time-wasting activities. If you see something that will likely impede the probability of success, lend a hand. If you obtain helpful information, funnel it to all involved; the ones you know and like and the ones you don't.

Build up people, and encourage them to think outside the norm. Express satisfaction with their work and the results they are achieving. Give lots of "Atta-boy," "Good job," and "Glad you're on my team" feedback as you get what you want and they get closer to the goal. Give them credit for whatever is going well; take responsibility when things don't go well. As one CEO told me, "You have to take any bullets yourself." You don't want to place blame for failure on anyone else. Taking it yourself lets you also take the initiative to correct the situation.

When they don't meet the expectations that you've previously laid out, go back and make your expectations clearer.

Occasionally an individual goes "off the deep end," getting in over her head, and you have to get on her case. If a person is wrong or misguided in her approach, thinking, or decision making, she should be told right away. The great payoff for separating your acceptance of character and motivation from your assessment of people's work is that it frees you to talk about and correct behavior. You correct the behavior, not the person. If someone told you, "Your report was lousy, and you need to redo it," sure, you'd be a little miffed, but your reaction would be mild compared to how you would feel if you were told, "Your report was lousy. I think you were dishonest in your evaluation. I wonder about your loyalty. I think you just wanted to put something out there so you could leave early and go cattin' around."

Don't change your demeanor. Speak candidly and calmly, without using incendiary words about the person's character, motive, or morals, Stick to his job performance.

If you don't like a coworker's or boss's actions or behavior, say so in a manner that doesn't criticize character or motive. Don't carry disgruntled or negative mental baggage with you. Let your opinion out; put your thinking on the table, there for discussion and consideration. Don't rely on a cascade effect and expect others to pass the word down for you. Get what you want to make clear out in the open as fast as possible. It's easier to live the other way of holding disagreement, discord, and conflict in, but doing so has its limits. The friction will come out sometime. You and others won't blow up if you let controversy out a little bit at a time. People don't know how to change unless you let disagreement out. Nicely nag them with explanations, examples, and stories to get them to do what they need to do. Don't be easy on them. Give them all the tools you can to discover how to improve behavior on their own.

Do not withdraw acceptance or withhold approval pending behavior changes. That's what a bad teacher or a mom and dad do, and it messes up their kids. Refrain from using "You always" or "You never" statements because the minute you use those words, the problem turns into personal criticism. "Your presentation disappointed me" is less offensive than "You always disappoint me in your presentations."

Repeat what you want, what you'll tolerate, and what is a deal breaker.

Do not allow:

- *Upward delegation*, for example, throwing the decision back onto you.
- *Malicious obedience*, for example, acting as if you obey and adhere with your outside demeanor but inside your head deciding not to—the maliciousness comes from your purposeful deceit.
- *Malicious disobedience*, for example, blatantly refusing to do as directed.

As a leader, your job is to do part of your boss's job, but not your subordinates' jobs. Paul Schlossberg, president of D/FW Consulting, writes this:

> When one has individuals directly assigned, it is essential to be a teacher, mentor, positive critic, and advocate for their personal and career growth. The feedback process should be structured and organized. This also demands that one must have the confidence to delegate and then get out of their way so that they can learn and grow. Give them room to do fully completed work.

Accept that most work is going to be a compromise, and you'll never get things done exactly the way you want. Their work will seldom be good enough for you, and they'll make mistakes. You're going to have to let some things go.

Talk about behavior once, then twice, and a third time: "This is the third time we've talked about this. I want this _____, not this _____. What part haven't I made clear?" Do not say, "What part don't you understand?" Also, don't talk to people in a toxic way: with a disproving facial expression, with a harsh tone of voice, or with sharp words. Instead, stick with the pass-the-salt tone, slight smile, and carefully chosen words.

Tell them, again, and again, and again as necessary, what you want and what you don't want, and do so in a neutral, nonjudgmental frame of mind: "You may not have understood from my direction, but here it is: you need to be five minutes early, not five minutes late. Got it, kiddo?" (All said with a neutral expression, a calm tone of voice, and an easy smile.) Don't imply that anything is wrong with the person. If the lateness is repeated, ask with the same calm tone and facial expression: "Do you want a job where you don't have to come in five minutes early? Is that job here, or is it elsewhere?"

Set an example, set expectations, state consequences for not meeting expected behavior, and enforce them. Then step back, and let them figure out the way. As one CEO told me, "Give people the job they aren't ready for so they can learn."

People work hard if you have goodwill for them.

The performance, ethics, attitude, and accountability you want to see in others start with you. Doing stellar work that sets you apart from others who put in less time, effort, and attention is one differentiator. But a bigger one that makes the CEO difference is when your manner causes others to do well too. Your number one job as a human being, in my experience, is to do all you can to maintain the self-esteem of others. If you do what you can to make them feel good about you, they will "walk on coals" for you, meaning they'll give you their all-out effort. All it takes for you to maintain their self-esteem is to accept who they are—that is, accept their character, motive, and ability. Don't judge, critique, or attack. Set clear work expectations, and state that you will hold them to the standard you set. Then hold them and yourself to that standard consistently.

CONCLUSION

MY DEFINITION of hell: you are on your deathbed, and someone brings in a flash drive, sticks it into your laptop, and shows you a video of all you could have done and could have been in your life—all the things you could have accomplished but you didn't go for. To that end, I'm always striving to do more and do better. I think you must feel the same way.

So this is what I hope you get out of my book: tangible steps to differentiate yourself, the know-how to do more than you thought you could, a friendly cajole and provocation to be your best, and permission to behave differently than your mom and dad taught you (if necessary).

If you're not already confident and optimistic, I also hope you become more self-aware and change how you view yourself. Being positive will cause you to be a more effective, persuasive, and attuned communicator. This book should also provide better coping methods, so that you feel comfortable in situations in which you previously felt uncomfortable. I want this book to inspire you to avoid wasting time in elevating your presence in the world for your own sake while forgetting the effect on others (the effect you have on others is imperative!). I also want you to consistently present yourself in a way that people are receptive to.

And, finally, I hope you have the knowledge that you can do all this.

There are two kinds of people who read these types of books: (1) those who will take the advice and run with it, and (2) those who won't. If you're in the first group, you will differentiate yourself.

It doesn't take that much to be exceptional. It just takes doing whatever you're doing in a way that is a little more special and enhanced than the rest.

If you consider the advice given in this book, you will see an over-riding pattern: to intelligently observe what most people do and then don't do that; do the opposite. Instead of giving an obvious answer to a problem, taking a typical route, doing what most people do, come up with something different: go a new way around it; break the pattern, color outside the lines; think outside the bun; be countercyclical and go against prevailing wisdom; do things in a novel way; and break a routine in an unexpected way. If you have even a whiff of "Everybody else is doing it . . . we've always done it this way," steer clear.

Instead of:

- Fitting in, stand out.
- Being negative, be positive and optimistic.
- Feeling inadequate, feel broadly adequate.
- Succumbing to temptation to allow a mistruth, speak up with honesty.
- Being insecure, be confident.
- Being judgmental, be approving and accepting.
- Being self-serving, be other oriented too.
- Slumping, slouching, and schlepping, stand tall and straight.
- Frowning, have an open mouth and genial face.
- Being a "yes" person, smartly argue with your boss.
- Learning more about your specialty, learn things totally unrelated.
- Doing only your job, go find people to help with their job.
- Seeking out a new mentor, seek to be a new mentor to someone else.
- Sending an e-mail, send a handwritten note or go walk and talk eyeball to eyeball.
- Avoiding conflict, be the peace broker.
- Being introverted, force yourself to engage with strangers.
- Hanging with people you relate to, hang with people you don't relate to.
- Rushing, slow down.
- Waiting, initiate before you're ready.

- Being part of a tribe, be alone.
- Being superserious, inject humor.
- Following the norm, avoid conformity.
- Playing by the rules, break some.
- Avoiding problems, seek them out.
- Procrastinating, take action and develop.
- Fearing mistakes, go for it and learn.
- Doing the job you're paid to do, do more.
- Dispensing data, really connect and bond in your communication.
- Judging, give acceptance.
- Speaking, shut up.
- Keeping quiet, speak up.
- Telling all you know, ask.
- Spewing facts and figures, tell a story.
- Making this all about your doing well, make it about others' doing well.

We're all unfinished people, and that is what is so exciting, fascinating, and freeing. All of us can do more and do better. Time in this world is limited, but things you can do in that time are not.

There are no incompetent people, only lazy ones.

Many people have helped me learn an effective way to go about my business in the world. I hope from the many conversations that have helped me, they also help you.

INDEX

ABOUT THE AUTHOR

D. A. (Debra) Benton has been helping great individuals and organizations get even better for more than 20 years. Just as exceptional athletes rely on excellent coaching to hone their skills, Debra's clients rely on her advice to advance their careers. She focuses on what is truly important to convert clients and their organizations from a vision of what they want to be to the reality of actually being it. TopCEOCoaches .com ranks her in the world's top 10 CEO coaches in the world, noting she is the top female. As a conference keynote speaker, Debra is routinely rated in the top 2 percent. Her client list reads like a *Who's Who* of executives in companies ranging from Microsoft, McDonald's, Kraft, American Express, Merrill Lynch, United Airlines, and PricewaterhouseCoopers to those in the Washington Beltway and the U.S. Border Patrol.

Debra is an award-winning and bestselling business author of 10 books, including *The Virtual Executive* and *CEO Material*. She has written for the *Harvard Business Review*, the *Wall Street Journal*, *Bloomberg Businessweek*, and *Fast Company*. She has been featured in *USA Today*, *Fortune*, the *New York Times*, and *Time* magazine. In addition, she has appeared on the *Today* show, *Good Morning America*, CNN, and has been interviewed by Diane Sawyer for *CBS This Morning*. To learn more about Debra's advising leaders, coaching, facilitating workshops, and speaking, please visit **www.debrabenton.com**.